Neural Networks with Python

Design CNNs, Transformers, GANs and capsule networks using tensorflow and keras

Mei Wong

GitforGits™
ASIAN PUBLISHING HOUSE

Published by: GitforGits
Publisher: Sonal Dhandre
www.gitforgits.com
support@gitforgits.com

Printed in India

First Printing: November 2023

ISBN: 978-8119177486

Cover Design by: Kitten Publishing

Prologue

Welcome to your journey into the heart of neural networks! If you're reading this, you're probably as fascinated by machine learning and AI as I am, and you're keen to get your hands dirty with real code. Trust me, you've picked the right book. We're going to dive deep into the world of neural networks, using Python as our trusty tool and TensorFlow and Keras as our sidekicks.

You know how sometimes machine learning feels like this huge, intimidating subject? I get it; I've been there. That's why the first thing we'll do is break it down to its basics. We'll look at why Python is the go-to language for all things machine learning. And don't worry if setting up programming environments isn't your strong suit; I've got your back. We'll go step by step to make sure you've got all you need to get started.

We shall learn about what makes this book different. You won't just be reading about neural networks; you'll be building them. We start simple with Feedforward and Convolutional Neural Networks. But we'll quickly get into the cooler stuff—Recurrent Neural Networks, Generative Adversarial Networks, Transformers, and even some next-level networks like Capsule Networks. You'll not only understand what these are but also learn how to build them from scratch. And the best part? You'll be working on real-world projects using actual datasets. Yep, you heard that right!

But hey, nobody said neural networks are a walk in the park. There are challenges, obstacles, and head-scratching moments. That's part of the fun, right? What's unique about this book is that we'll also focus on the problems you might face while building these networks. We'll look at how to troubleshoot them and even how to fine-tune your models. By the end of it, you won't just know how to build a neural network; you'll know what to do when things don't go as planned.

So here's the deal: if you're up for a rollercoaster ride through the incredible world of neural networks, hold tight. Grab a cup of coffee, open up your favorite code editor, and let's get started. I promise it's going to be an exciting journey!

Content

Preface

"Neural Networks with Python" is a pragmatic and self-learning book for anyone looking to master the art of neural network development, whether you're a seasoned data scientist or new to the field. This book offers a comprehensive yet accessible dive into the complex realm of neural networks, all through the lens of Python—one of the most powerful tools in the machine learning ecosystem.

This book is a hands-on journey that takes you from the foundational basics to the advanced techniques, with real-world examples and datasets at every turn. Starting with Python essentials, we lay down the groundwork to ensure a smooth experience throughout the book. From there, we explore a variety of neural network architectures—Feedforward, Convolutional, Recurrent Neural Networks, Generative Adversarial Networks, Transformers, and Capsule Networks. Each architecture is dissected, understood, and then brought to life with practical examples.

What sets this book apart is its focus on the challenges and intricacies of building and fine-tuning neural networks. You'll learn not just how to build these networks, but also how to make them efficient and effective. The book provides a rich toolkit of troubleshooting techniques, helping you navigate through common pitfalls and bottlenecks. The result? By the end of this book, you'll be well-equipped to develop neural networks that are optimized, robust, and tailored to any problem statement.

The key outcome of this book is the empowerment it provides. You won't be just a passive learner; you'll become an active practitioner capable of tackling a wide array of machine learning challenges. "Neural Networks with Python" is your perfect learner in becoming the machine learning expert you've always aspired to be. With this book in hand, you're not just learning you're doing, and that's where true mastery lies.

In this book you will learn how to:

- Master Python for machine learning, from setup to complex models.
- Gain flexibility with diverse neural network architectures for various problems.
- Hands-on experience in building, training, and fine-tuning neural networks.
- Learn strategic approaches for troubleshooting and optimizing neural models.
- Grasp advanced topics like autoencoders, capsule networks, and attention mechanisms.
- Acquire skills in crucial data preprocessing and augmentation techniques.

- Understand and apply optimization techniques and hyperparameter tuning.
- Implement an end-to-end machine learning project, from data to deployment.

GitforGits

Prerequisites

All you need is to hold a good understanding of python scripting with active interest in learning neural networks, machine learning modeling and use of statistical techniques. And, there is nothing to worry as every individual chapter tries to give you a soft recap on key topics and concepts very oftenly throughout the book.

Codes Usage

Are you in need of some helpful code examples to assist you in your programming and documentation? Look no further! Our book offers a wealth of supplemental material, including code examples and exercises.

Not only is this book here to aid you in getting your job done, but you have our permission to use the example code in your programs and documentation. However, please note that if you are reproducing a significant portion of the code, we do require you to contact us for permission.

But don't worry, using several chunks of code from this book in your program or answering a question by citing our book and quoting example code does not require permission. But if you do choose to give credit, an attribution typically includes the title, author, publisher, and ISBN. For example, "Neural Networks with Python by Mei Wong".

If you are unsure whether your intended use of the code examples falls under fair use or the permissions outlined above, please do not hesitate to reach out to us at support@gitforgits.com.

We are happy to assist and clarify any concerns.

Acknowledgement

I owe a tremendous debt of gratitude to GitforGits, for their unflagging enthusiasm and wise counsel throughout the entire process of writing this book. Their knowledge and careful editing helped make sure the piece was useful for people of all reading levels and comprehension skills. In addition, I'd like to thank everyone involved in the publishing process for their efforts in making this book a reality. Their efforts, from copyediting to advertising, made the project what it is today.

Finally, I'd like to express my gratitude to everyone who has shown me unconditional love and encouragement throughout my life. Their support was crucial to the completion of this book. I appreciate your help with this endeavour and your continued interest in my career.

Chapter 1: Python, Tensorflow, and your First Neural Network

Machine Learning and Rise of Python Tools

Machine learning has undergone a phenomenal surge in popularity over the last decade, becoming an integral part of various industries, from healthcare and finance to entertainment and self-driving vehicles. This remarkable growth is a direct result of computational advancements and the availability of vast amounts of data. However, the true enabler of this revolution has been the development of sophisticated programming tools designed to simplify the complexities of machine learning algorithms. Python has emerged as the leading language in this space, providing a rich ecosystem for scientific computing and machine learning. Tools like TensorFlow, Keras, and PyTorch have become the linchpins of modern machine learning, offering flexible platforms for designing, training, and deploying models.

TensorFlow, developed by Google Brain, provides a comprehensive suite of functionalities needed for various machine learning tasks. It has become particularly popular for deep learning due to its scalability and efficiency. The core of TensorFlow is based on data flow graphs, which allow complex computations to be distributed across multiple CPUs or GPUs seamlessly. This modular structure makes it easy to deploy TensorFlow models to diverse environments, from a laptop to large server clusters. The eager execution feature allows for immediate evaluation of operations, making TensorFlow an ideal choice for interactive experimentation and debugging. For those familiar with Python and NumPy, TensorFlow provides a natural transition to building machine learning models using familiar array operations. The wide adoption of TensorFlow is also due to its rich ecosystem of tools like TensorFlow Serving for deployment, TensorFlow Lite for mobile development, and TensorFlow.js for web applications. This end-to-end support makes TensorFlow a versatile choice for various machine learning needs.

Keras, which can run on top of TensorFlow, offers a simpler interface and is ideal for beginners. It uses high-level building blocks like layers and models which simplify the coding process. The modular design principles make it extremely intuitive to construct neural networks of varying complexity. Keras supports convolutional and recurrent networks out of the box, along with wide-ranging options for activation functions, regularizers, optimizers and more. The simple APIs can get complex models up and running quickly, allowing rapid prototyping and experimentation. Keras also plays well with TensorFlow features like distributed training and TPU support. The overall experience enables fast transition from idea to implementation, making Keras a popular starting point for machine learning enthusiasts and experts alike.

PyTorch, developed by Facebook's AI Research Lab, provides an alternative to TensorFlow, offering dynamic computation graphs that are particularly useful for research. The key difference lies in its define-by-run approach compared to TensorFlow's static graph paradigm. This allows PyTorch models to adapt and change during runtime, making iterative model design effortless. Researchers can build prototypes quickly, modify architectures and try out new ideas with minimal code changes. Combined with Pythonic syntax and GPU acceleration, PyTorch provides the flexibility needed for machine learning research. The eager evaluation mode in PyTorch also simplifies debugging and inspection. PyTorch supports production deployment via TorchScript and integrates well with Python data science stacks. The active ecosystem includes tools for computer vision, natural language processing and reinforcement learning. PyTorch adoption continues to grow, especially in academic circles, due to its focus on research.

Setting up a robust machine learning development environment is crucial for the success of any machine learning project. The development environment is not just a collection of tools and libraries; it's a cohesive framework where data exploration, feature engineering, model development, training, evaluation, and deployment occur. TensorFlow and Keras offer more than just a programming interface; they offer an environment where developers can implement, test, and iterate models efficiently. For instance, TensorFlow provides TensorBoard for visualizing metrics like loss and accuracy during training runs. Debugging options like tf.GradientTape allow inspection of gradient flows during backpropagation. TensorFlow Data Validation can analyze training data for errors and biases. Keras also simplifies many aspects of workflow including model serialization, callbacks for custom training logic and built-in support for transfer learning.

A well-structured development environment helps in maintaining consistency across various stages of the machine learning pipeline, ensuring that the transition from development to production is smooth and devoid of any hiccups. The cloud-based AI Platform by Google Cloud integrates tightly with TensorFlow, enabling scalable training on vast compute resources. Deployed models can be monitored, updated, and managed using tools like Cloud Machine Learning Engine. Amazon SageMaker provides similar capabilities for end-to-end machine learning on AWS. These managed platforms eliminate infrastructure overheads associated with large-scale model development.

In the world of machine learning, the development environment extends beyond the programming language and libraries to include data storage solutions, version control systems, and even cloud computing resources for scalable model training. Efficient data management is essential for handling large datasets, and version control is indispensable for team collaborations. TensorFlow Datasets and

Keras provide standard interfaces for working with datasets residing on disk or in cloud storage. Integrating git with Jupyter notebooks helps track experiments and code changes during iterative development. Cloud-based notebooks simplify sharing and provide built-in versioning. Integrating these elements into a unified environment streamlines the workflow, making it easier to track changes, roll back to previous model versions, and share work among team members.

Furthermore, with the advent of DevOps practices in machine learning, or MLOps, the development environment becomes a part of a larger ecosystem that includes continuous integration, automated testing, and continuous deployment. TensorFlow Extended and KerasTuner enable standardized model evaluation and hyperparameter tuning. CI/CD pipelines can package models and automate rollouts. A well-configured development environment is, therefore, not a luxury but a necessity for successful machine learning projects. The Python machine learning stack has evolved into a mature platform that enables both productivity and collaboration throughout the machine learning lifecycle.

Python Environment Setup on Linux

Installing Python

We shall begin by setting up Python. Although many Linux distributions come pre-installed with Python, it's essential to ensure you have the latest version for your machine learning endeavors. One way to install or upgrade Python on Linux is by using the package manager specific to your distribution. For Ubuntu or Debian-based systems, the package manager is APT (Advanced Package Tool), whereas, for Fedora, you'd use dnf, and for CentOS, it's yum.

For instance, on an Ubuntu system, you can install Python by opening your terminal and executing the following commands:

```
sudo apt update
sudo apt install python3
```

This will install the latest version of Python 3 available in the repositories. The apt update command refreshes the package index before installing Python.

An alternative method is to use pyenv, which allows multiple Python versions to be installed side by side. After installing pyenv using your package manager, you can install a specific Python version as follows:

```
pyenv install 3.12
pyenv global 3.12
```

This will download and set Python 3.12 as the global Python version. Pyenv is useful for testing code against different Python versions.

Once Python is installed, you can verify the version from the terminal by running:

```
python3 --version
```

This step ensures that you have a foundational programming language that has become the mainstay of various machine learning and data science projects. Python's versatility, ease of use, and wide range of libraries make it an indispensable tool in your machine learning journey.

Installing Python Dependencies

After installing Python, the next step is to set up the associated dependencies. Python's rich ecosystem includes numerous libraries and frameworks that simplify the machine learning workflow, from data preprocessing and visualization to model training and evaluation. Two of the most important libraries that you'll frequently use are NumPy for numerical operations and Pandas for data manipulation. You can install these libraries using Python's package manager, pip. If pip is not installed, you can install it using sudo apt install python3-pip for Ubuntu. Once pip is ready, install NumPy and Pandas by executing:

```
pip3 install numpy pandas
```

The pip3 install command fetches the specified packages and installs them, making it incredibly easy to manage Python libraries. With NumPy and Pandas installed, you've taken a significant step towards creating a robust machine learning environment. These libraries are foundational blocks for data manipulation and numerical computation in Python, and you'll find yourself using them extensively as you delve deeper into machine learning.

Setting up Integrated Development Environment (IDE)

The last piece of the puzzle is setting up an Integrated Development Environment (IDE) for writing and managing your Python scripts. While you can certainly use a simple text editor for coding, an IDE offers many advantages like code completion, debugging, and version control. One of the most widely used IDEs for Python development is Visual Studio Code (VS Code). You can download it from the official website or install it via the package manager. For Ubuntu, the installation command would be:

```
sudo apt install code
```

Once installed, you can launch VS Code from the terminal by typing code. You can also install the Python extension for VS Code to get additional Python-specific features. With an IDE like VS Code, you not only get a platform for writing code but also a range of tools that assist in debugging, version control, and even deployment. Setting up a suitable IDE is the final step in creating a conducive development environment for machine learning. With Python, essential libraries, and an IDE installed, you're well-equipped to start your machine learning journey.

Verification of Environment Setup

Importance of Verification

Verifying your Python environment with a simple script serves multiple purposes. First, it ensures that Python is correctly installed and accessible from your IDE. Second, it offers a glimpse into the development workflow, from writing and saving code to executing it in the terminal or directly within the IDE. Lastly, this initial hands-on experience serves as a confidence booster, a small but significant step that mentally prepares you for the more complex machine learning projects ahead. It's akin to a pilot doing a pre-flight check; it's a simple procedure but one that can catch issues before they escalate into more significant problems. Therefore, writing a basic Python script is a useful exercise to confirm that you've correctly set up your development environment.

Writing the Classic 'Hello, World!'

When learning a new programming language, writing your first "Hello, World!" program is a big milestone. It's a tradition that goes back decades to the early days of coding. The goal is simple - get the computer to print a friendly greeting to the screen. This shows that you've got your tools set up right and can start writing real programs.

It's kind of like a test drive when you get a new car. Before hitting the open road, you drive around the block first to make sure everything is working. "Hello, World!" is your quick spin around the programming neighborhood.

We shall try it in Python. First, open up your IDE, which is probably Visual Studio Code if you followed the previous steps. Create a new file called hello_world.py.

In this file, add one line:

```
print("Hello, World!")
```

That prints our greeting. Save the file. Now open terminal and use the cd command to navigate to the folder where you saved hello_world.py. Type python3 hello_world.py and hit Enter to run it.

If all goes well, you should see the comforting words "Hello, World!" displayed. It's working! This confirms Python is installed correctly and your IDE can edit, save, and run scripts.

While it seems simple, getting this basic program running is an important milestone. It means you can now start coding in Python with confidence. The training wheels are off! "Hello, World!" might not be flashy, but it tests the core parts of your dev environment without much else to break. It's like a handshake greeting you as you embark on your Python programming adventure.

Understanding Components of Script

When learning to code, that first "Hello, World!" script marks a big milestone. We shall break it down to see what makes it tick, even though it's just one line.

The print() function is built into Python to display output on screen. We pass it a string, or text in quotes, to print. Python uses either single or double quotes for strings, which can have letters, numbers, and symbols. So print() takes our "Hello, World!" string and shows it. This one line covers some core programming ideas - functions, data types, and console output. As you get into machine learning, you'll build on these basics with more advanced functions, data structures, and output methods. But remember, the fancy algorithms rely on these simple foundations.

Why Start Simple?

Starting with a simple script gives you a chance to learn the coding environment itself before tackling complex code. You can get familiar with the IDE, like creating and managing files. Practice running scripts from terminal. These are crucial skills for any programming, especially machine learning with loads of files, libraries, and dependencies. When it's second nature, you can focus on problem-solving and algorithms. A quick win like "Hello, World!" shows you can write a complete, working program in just a few minutes. Even as projects grow in scope, it's motivating to remember they start small, one line at a time.

From Simple to Complex

Once you get that first script running, you're ready for bigger things! But keep in mind complexity includes more than fancy algorithms - it's also about process. Writing, testing, debugging and deploying code gets more intricate with data prep, model training, metrics, and other machine learning components. But the core ideas stay the same - write code, test it, fix it, run it. "Hello, World!" is the first step on an rewarding journey of problem-solving and innovation.

Think of it like learning to drive. You start by driving around the block just to make sure everything works. Then you take on highways, traffic, and long trips. With programming, you need to make sure the basics work before launching into advanced projects.

By getting that simple program running, you've verified Python is installed properly and you can edit, save, and execute scripts. You also picked up the core ideas like functions, strings, and printing output. These basics will serve you well as you delve into machine learning, giving you the foundation to tackle any problem. The most complex code is still built on simple principles.

So pat yourself on the back - you've joined generations of programmers who got their start with "Hello, World!". It's a rite of passage, initiating you into the world of coding, where creativity and persistence pay off. The journey ahead will be challenging but rewarding. And one day, when you've mastered machine learning, you can look back fondly at that simple script that started it all.

Introduction to TensorFlow

Advent of TensorFlow

TensorFlow has undoubtedly emerged as one of the most significant and comprehensive platforms for machine learning and particularly for deep learning tasks. Developed by the Google Brain team and released in 2015 as an open-source project, TensorFlow was designed to be flexible, robust, and capable of serving both research and production needs. Its initial appeal stemmed from its computational graph abstraction, which allows users to define complex mathematical operations as directed graphs. This graph-based approach provided the framework for optimized and parallel computations, an essential requirement for handling the immense computational needs of deep learning models.

TensorFlow's Capabilities

What really sets TensorFlow apart is that it goes way beyond basic neural networks. It's like a full workshop of tools and libraries covering all aspects of machine learning. TensorFlow can handle everything from classic algorithms like classification and regression to cutting-edge deep learning models.

For deep learning, TensorFlow has first-class support for state-of-the-art architectures like CNNs for computer vision, RNNs and LSTMs for sequences like text and audio, and Transformers which have revolutionized natural language processing. TensorFlow also readily scales across multiple GPUs and servers, making it great for both small experiments and massive industrial applications. Another killer feature is TensorBoard, TensorFlow's visualization toolkit. Being able to monitor training runs, visualize neural network graphs, and debug model internals is invaluable. The TensorFlow ecosystem even extends to mobile and embedded devices, allowing deployment of models virtually anywhere. This makes it easy to take machine learning from research to real-world production use cases.

TensorFlow's impact on both academics and industry is significant. In research, it's enabled pushing boundaries on what neural networks can achieve. Groundbreaking papers at top conferences in NLP, computer vision, and reinforcement learning often use TensorFlow for implementing novel techniques. Its flexibility suits the dynamic nature of research, where you want to rapidly prototype and experiment. Industrially, TensorFlow powers many innovative products and services today. For example, Google uses it for voice recognition in Assistant and image recognition for Photos. It also enables machine learning models behind Search, YouTube recommendations, and more. Beyond Google, it's been adopted across healthcare, automotive, finance, and other sectors. With easy scaling and deployment, TensorFlow is ideal for enterprises to integrate machine learning into real applications.

What does the future look like for TensorFlow? Exciting, with new developments focused on speed, scalability, and accessibility. Cutting-edge innovations like TensorFlow Quantum for quantum machine learning and TensorFlow Federated for decentralized training point to the next frontiers of ML. With its proven track record, vibrant community, and wide academic and industry adoption, TensorFlow is firmly established as a pillar of the ever-evolving machine learning landscape. For newcomers, TensorFlow's vast capabilities can seem daunting at first. But the platform is flexible enough for both amateurs tinkering with machine learning and seasoned experts pushing boundaries. The many pre-built models and tutorials make it easy to get started. At the same time, access to advanced features ensures you won't outgrow TensorFlow as your skills improve. TensorFlow didn't become a machine learning juggernaut overnight. Its success stems from solving real problems faced by practitioners, researchers, and students in a practical way.

TensorFlow Basics

Tensor

At the heart of TensorFlow are tensors, which are multi-dimensional arrays that serve as the basic building blocks for creating neural networks and machine learning models. The name "TensorFlow" itself is derived from the operations that neural networks perform on tensors. Understanding tensors is crucial for grasping how data flows and transforms within a TensorFlow program.

A tensor has three primary attributes: rank, shape, and type. The rank of a tensor refers to the number of dimensions it has. For instance, a scalar has a rank of 0, a vector has a rank of 1, a matrix has a rank of 2, and so on. The shape of a tensor defines the length of each dimension, and the type specifies the data type of the tensor elements, such as float32, int32, etc. These attributes provide a comprehensive way to describe any form of data, from a single number to a complex multi-dimensional array. Understanding the nature and capabilities of tensors is the first step in harnessing the power of TensorFlow for machine learning tasks.

TensorFlow Graphs and Sessions

Once you understand tensors, the next foundational concept is the computational graph, a series of TensorFlow operations arranged as nodes in a graph. Each node in the graph represents an operation that takes zero or more tensors as input and produces a tensor as output. This graph-based approach enables TensorFlow to offload computations to different hardware accelerators like GPUs and TPUs, thereby optimizing performance. Initially, the graph is like a blueprint, describing the order and computation but not executing anything.

To run the operations, you need to create a TensorFlow session that allocates resources and executes the graph. The session feeds data into the graph and retrieves the output, allowing you to perform computations and train models. Understanding how graphs and sessions work together is essential for using TensorFlow efficiently, as they serve as the execution environment for your machine learning models.

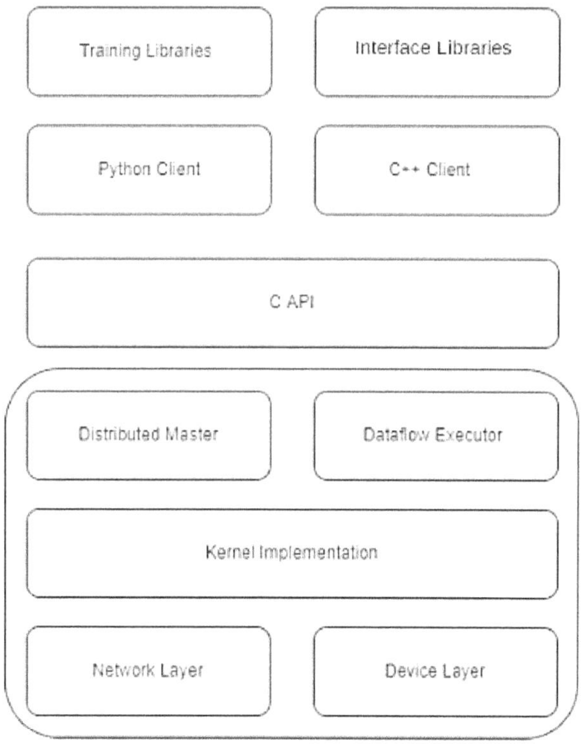

Fig 1.1 TensorFlow Architecture

Gradient Descent and Backpropagation

When it comes to training machine learning models, especially neural networks, one of the most crucial algorithms you'll encounter in TensorFlow is Gradient Descent. The algorithm iteratively adjusts the model's parameters to minimize the error between the predicted and actual outcomes. The process of computing these parameter adjustments efficiently is known as backpropagation.

In TensorFlow, you can implement Gradient Descent and backpropagation without having to delve into the intricate mathematical details. TensorFlow's automatic differentiation engine takes care of the complex calculus for you. You simply define the model architecture, specify the loss function, and TensorFlow handles the gradients. This abstraction allows you to focus on designing better models rather than getting entangled in the underlying math. However, having a conceptual understanding of Gradient Descent and backpropagation will provide you with insights into how the model learns from data, which is invaluable for debugging and optimizing your models.

'Eager Execution' Feature

TensorFlow 2.x introduced a significant feature called Eager Execution, which allows operations to compute immediately as they are called, instead of building a computational graph to run later. This makes TensorFlow more intuitive and easier to debug, bringing it more in line with the way Python generally works. While the graph-based approach is excellent for optimization and deployment, eager execution simplifies the development and testing process. It allows you to run TensorFlow operations instantly and inspect the output, making it easier to debug models and understand the flow of tensors in your program. This is particularly beneficial for beginners and researchers who are experimenting with new models, as it offers a more straightforward, Pythonic way of developing TensorFlow applications.

High-level and Low-level APIs

TensorFlow provides both high-level and low-level APIs to cater to different needs. The high-level APIs, like Keras, offer an easier entry point for beginners. With just a few lines of code, you can define and train a neural network. However, this simplicity comes at the cost of customizability. On the other hand, TensorFlow's low-level APIs give you complete control over the model architecture, but they require a deeper understanding of TensorFlow's inner workings. Being aware of the capabilities and limitations of these APIs is crucial for effectively using TensorFlow. Depending on your project's needs, you may start with high-level APIs for rapid prototyping and then switch to low-level APIs for fine-grained control during the optimization phase.

Introduction to Keras and Its Capabilities

Genesis of Keras

Keras burst onto the machine learning scene as an independent project with a bold vision - to create a powerful yet easy-to-use neural network toolkit. Its founder, François Chollet, wanted to build an API that enabled fast experimentation and rapid prototyping. But it also had to be flexible enough for researchers and engineers to design state-of-the-art models. This combination of simplicity and extensibility hit a sweet spot in the machine learning community. Keras gained a loyal following among practitioners who appreciated its focus on usability.

Keras Capabilities

Keras offers a range of functionalities tailored to enable quick model development. Its primary advantage lies in its simplicity and ease of use, without compromising on the capacity for customization. It provides simple APIs for defining layers, setting up optimizers, and compiling models. Various built-in layers are available for creating diverse neural network architectures, from basic feedforward networks to complex structures like convolutional and recurrent neural networks. One of Keras' most notable features is its "Sequential" and "Functional" APIs for building models. While the Sequential API allows for the straightforward stacking of layers, the Functional API offers more flexibility, enabling the creation of complex models with multiple inputs or outputs and shared layers. Additionally, Keras also provides utilities for data preprocessing, model evaluation, and hyperparameter tuning, making it a comprehensive toolkit for the entire machine learning pipeline.

Keras has become a go-to tool for researchers and industry professionals alike, particularly in the field of deep learning. In academia, it has been used to prototype novel algorithms and architectures, often serving as the initial platform for experiments that later transition to more complex implementations. Numerous research papers featuring Keras have been published in top machine learning conferences, highlighting its role in advancing the state of the art in areas like computer vision, natural language processing, and reinforcement learning. Its ease of use enables researchers to focus on the conceptual and theoretical aspects of their work, without getting bogged down by the intricacies of model implementation.

In the industrial sector, Keras has facilitated the rapid deployment of machine learning models in various applications such as predictive maintenance, recommendation systems, and natural language interfaces. Companies like Uber have used Keras for developing their machine learning models, appreciating its balance of simplicity and power. Startups and established tech giants alike find Keras to be a reliable solution for quickly testing ideas and deploying effective machine learning systems. It's the ease and speed of model development in Keras that make it particularly useful for businesses that need to operate in agile and dynamic environments.

Keras for TensorFlow Ecosystem

Integrating Keras as TensorFlow's high-level API supercharged its capabilities and adoption. This tag-team combination gives you Keras's simplicity with TensorFlow's performance and scalability. Models created in Keras can also be converted to TensorFlow, enabling a smooth path from prototyping to production. Together, they provide a solution for machine learning tasks ranging from simple to extremely complex with millions of parameters.

Think of Keras like a user-friendly remote control for operating TensorFlow under the hood. Just like switching TV channels, you can build and train models without worrying about the intricate internals. Keras has made state-of-the-art machine learning more accessible to practitioners who care more about applying ML than the mathematical details. At the same time, it doesn't constrain experts who want to customize and optimize their models.

The Keras ecosystem continues to expand with new features and third-party extensions. Active forums and tutorials foster a growing community. As machine learning advances, tools that mitigate complexity become increasingly valuable. Keras delivers on this need for an interface balancing simplicity and customizability.

For beginners, Keras provides a gentle introduction to neural networks. As users gain proficiency, they find Keras flexible enough to not limit them. This broad accessibility fuels its popularity among students, researchers, and companies. Underneath its approachable interface, Keras is still incredibly capable at tackling real-world problems. Keras has been a game-changer for applied machine learning. Its design philosophy empowers users to be more productive and move fast. In the fast-paced world of ML where innovation happens quickly, Keras delivers the right abstractions that focus attention on the ideas rather than underlying code.

Synergy of Python, TensorFlow, and Keras

Python for Neural Networks

Python is the glue that binds together TensorFlow, Keras, and other pieces of the machine learning puzzle. Its simple yet powerful design makes Python a favorite among new learners and expert developers alike. When it comes to neural networks, Python plays multiple roles.

First, it acts as the host language for TensorFlow and Keras. Python's clean syntax, readability, and huge standard library provide a solid foundation for these frameworks. But Python contributes much more than just hosting abilities. It also offers libraries for data wrangling like Pandas and NumPy for scientific computing. These tools allow vital preprocessing and feature engineering before models are built. Specialized libraries like NLTK for natural language processing are also available. This rich ecosystem enables developers to focus on high-level model logic rather than mathematical details. In a way, Python provides the underlying data structures, algorithms, and programming logic needed by TensorFlow and Keras. It handles the nuts and bolts so you can operate at a higher level of abstraction. Python's versatility to work on everything from early data cleanup to late stage deployment makes it the perfect glue to bring the workflow together.

So while TensorFlow enables high-performance numerical calculation and Keras provides simplicity, Python plays an equally important role. It gives you the tools to transform raw data into useful inputs for training clever models. Python complements TensorFlow and Keras to provide a complete platform for building and deploying real-world machine learning applications.

TensorFlow's Computation Power

While Python provides the flexible glue, TensorFlow supplies the optimized heavy lifting critical for neural network computations. It introduces an environment specialized for the extensive mathematical operations needed to train models. TensorFlow enables efficient manipulation of tensors, the core data structures of neural networks.

Its computation graph paradigm allows developers to outline complex chains of operations symbolically before executing them. This graph representation enables extensive optimization under the hood so models can train faster. TensorFlow abstracts away gritty algorithm details so practitioners can instead focus on high-level model architecture and design. In addition, TensorFlow provides first-class support for distributed training across multiple CPUs and GPUs. This proves invaluable for large neural network models that demand massive computational resources. TensorFlow scales effortlessly from laptops to server clusters, enabling both small scale experimentation and production-level deployment. The framework also contains specialized libraries for domains like natural language processing, computer vision, and reinforcement learning.

The combination of Python for flexible data wrangling and TensorFlow for optimized computation establishes a powerful platform. While Python equips developers with an extensive toolset for real-world data preparation, TensorFlow allows efficient implementation of machine learning algorithms. Together, they enable practitioners to build sophisticated models that learn from messy real-world data. Python and TensorFlow complement each other to provide a scalable environment from prototype to production.

Keras Simplified Interface

While TensorFlow provides optimized computation, Keras acts as the user-friendly interface enabling rapid iteration. Keras simplifies the process of building deep learning models without sacrificing much control or performance. This makes Keras the perfect wrapper around TensorFlow's advanced capabilities.

For example, constructing a convolutional neural network for image classification requires significantly fewer lines of code in Keras compared to native TensorFlow. Keras provides simple, clean APIs for layers, activations, optimizers, and other components needed to assemble neural networks. This simplifies experimenting with different architectures to find what works best. The higher-level abstractions in Keras allow quicker iteration and testing of ideas. Moreover, Keras' simplicity often directly translates to faster development cycles and reduced debugging time. For many real-world projects, development speed and ease of use are just as crucial as computational performance. The improved productivity and tighter feedback loops enabled by Keras better equip teams to deliver machine learning systems on time. Its accessibility also opens up complex deep learning techniques to a broader community of developers, researchers, and data scientists.

Ultimately, Keras establishes a more intuitive interface to TensorFlow, without significantly compromising on capability. Just like a dashboard simplifies controlling a car's engine, Keras democratizes access to state-of-the-art deep learning for practitioners at any skill level. The combination of TensorFlow's optimizations and Keras' simplicity delivers the best of both worlds - high-performance and rapid iteration. Together, they provide both the tooling and abstractions needed to solve real-world problems with machine learning.

Integration and Interoperability

A key advantage of combining Python, TensorFlow, and Keras is the integrated workflow it enables for end-to-end model development. The components neatly complement each other to support the full pipeline - from data preparation to model deployment.

A project might use Python's Pandas for initial data gathering and cleansing. The preprocessed data then enters a TensorFlow workflow for feature engineering and tensor manipulation. Finally, Keras provides a simple yet powerful interface for rapidly assembling, training, and evaluating neural network models. This demonstrates how each tool plays a distinct yet synergistic role. Python handles raw data wrangling. TensorFlow enables optimized mathematical computation. And Keras simplifies model construction. Furthermore, the Keras integration into TensorFlow allows models to be saved and loaded in either format. This makes it easy to transition between high- and low-level implementations as needed.

Together, Python, TensorFlow, and Keras form a versatile machine learning toolkit applicable to diverse problems and skill levels. Python provides versatility and a vast ecosystem of libraries for all development needs. TensorFlow delivers optimized performance critical for numerical computations involved in neural networks. And Keras brings an intuitive interface to quickly iterate on models. This combination offers both accessibility and exceptional capabilities - a win-win for practitioners. The integrated workflow enables seamless end-to-end development while also giving flexibility to work at different abstraction levels.

Installation of TensorFlow and Keras

Python Package Manager and Virtual Environment

Before you get started with installing TensorFlow and Keras, think of setting up a virtual environment as creating a personalized workspace for your project. It's like having a separate desk for each project, so things don't get mixed up. You can easily set up this workspace using Python's venv module. Just go to your project folder and type python3 -m venv myenv, where 'myenv' is the name you pick for your workspace. To start using it, you'll need to 'activate' it. If you're on a Linux or macOS computer, type source myenv/bin/activate. On a Windows machine, you'll use myenv\Scripts\Activate. You'll know it's activated when you see its name in your terminal.

Installing TensorFlow

We shall learn about adding TensorFlow to your workspace. There are two main types: one that works best with your computer's central processing unit (CPU) and another that's optimized for graphics processing units (GPU). The CPU version is like a regular car—good for everyday tasks. The GPU version is more like a race car—built for speed and heavy-duty tasks, like training big neural networks. To install TensorFlow, you'll use Python's handy tool installer, pip. In your activated workspace, type pip install tensorflow for the CPU version. If you're looking to use the speedier GPU version, type pip install tensorflow-gpu. Just keep in mind, the GPU version needs some extra setup and compatible hardware, so you'll want to check the official guidelines to get all the details.

Verifying TensorFlow Installation

After the installation is complete, it's crucial to verify that TensorFlow has been successfully installed and is functioning as expected. You can run a simple Python script to validate your installation.

Open a Python shell within your virtual environment and enter the following commands:

```
import tensorflow as tf
print(tf.__version__)
```

If everything is set up correctly, this should print the version number of the installed TensorFlow package. This verification step is more than a ritual; it's a necessary measure to ensure that you've successfully created a stable development environment. Knowing that your installation is correct can save you from unpredictable errors and issues later on, allowing you to proceed with the development of your neural networks with confidence.

Installing Keras

Keras is now integrated into TensorFlow as its official high-level API, which means that when you install TensorFlow, you already have access to Keras. You can simply import Keras modules directly from TensorFlow without requiring a separate installation.

To verify that Keras is available, you can open a Python shell in your virtual environment and run:

```
from tensorflow import keras
print(keras.__version__)
```

This should display the Keras version, confirming that it's ready for use. Having Keras bundled with TensorFlow simplifies the process and ensures compatibility, as you don't have to worry about matching versions between TensorFlow and Keras. This integrated approach paves the way for a smoother and more streamlined development process, as you can easily switch between low-level TensorFlow operations and high-level Keras APIs as your project requirements evolve.

Once you've verified that both TensorFlow and Keras are successfully installed, it's important to keep them up to date. Both libraries are actively developed, with new features, improvements, and bug fixes being released regularly. To update TensorFlow and Keras, you can run pip install --upgrade tensorflow within your virtual environment.

Selection of Deep Learning Dataset

Introduction to MNIST Dataset

Think of the MNIST dataset as the "starter kit" for anyone diving into deep learning and neural networks. It's a big album of 70,000 black-and-white pictures of handwritten numbers from 0 to 9. These pictures are tiny, just 28x28 pixels each. The album is sorted into 60,000 pictures for practice and 10,000 for the final test. Because it's so commonly used, it's like the "pop quiz" everyone takes in the world of machine learning. It's simple enough for newbies but has enough twists and turns to let you try out different neural network designs. So, it's a great place to kick off our learning adventure, especially with so many guides and studies that use it.

Why is MNIST a Good Choice?

MNIST is a great fit for a book focused on teaching neural networks and deep learning. For starters, it's a well-rounded dataset, so you don't have to worry about it being skewed or unfair, which is great for newcomers. Also, while basic machine learning methods can do okay with it, deep learning can really shine by picking up the finer details in the handwriting. Plus, it's versatile. You can use it to learn about everything from straightforward neural networks to fancier setups like CNNs (think of these as specialized for image tasks) and even RNNs (good for things that have a sequence or order). So, MNIST is like a playground where you can both learn the basics and experiment with advanced stuff.

Loading MNIST Dataset

Importing Required Libraries

Before loading the MNIST dataset, you'll need to import the necessary libraries. Open your Python environment where you've installed TensorFlow and Keras. Import TensorFlow and Keras as follows:

```
import tensorflow as tf
from tensorflow.keras import datasets
```

Here, we're importing TensorFlow and specifically the datasets module from Keras, which contains utilities for loading several well-known datasets, including MNIST.

Downloading and Loading the Dataset

Keras provides a straightforward way to download and load the MNIST dataset through its datasets API. You can download and load the MNIST dataset as follows:

```
(train_images, train_labels), (test_images, test_labels) = datasets.mnist.load_data()
```

This command performs multiple tasks. It downloads the MNIST dataset, loads it into memory, and splits it into training and test sets. The images and labels for the training and test datasets are stored in train_images, train_labels, test_images, and test_labels, respectively.

Exploring Loaded Dataset

Once the dataset is loaded, it's good practice to explore it to understand its structure. You can check the shape of the training and test datasets to confirm that they've been loaded correctly:

```
print("Training images shape:", train_images.shape)
```

```
print("Training labels shape:", train_labels.shape)
print("Test images shape:", test_images.shape)
print("Test labels shape:", test_labels.shape)
```

This will output the dimensions of the image and label arrays, giving you a clearer understanding of the dataset you'll be working with. Normally, you'd also visualize some samples from the dataset, which is possible using Python libraries like Matplotlib, to get a sense of the kind of images you're dealing with. While the MNIST dataset is relatively clean, some preprocessing steps are generally advisable before training a neural network. These can include normalizing the image pixel values to a range of 0 to 1, and one-hot encoding the labels, among others. We will explore the preprocessing in the next section.

Understand Data Preprocessing

Essence of Data Preprocessing

Imagine you're a chef about to cook a complex dish. You wouldn't just throw all the ingredients into a pot without chopping, marinating, or seasoning, right? Similarly, in the world of neural networks, data preprocessing is like your kitchen prep work. It's all about taking your raw ingredients—your data—and getting it ready for the main event: training your neural network model.

Why is this step so vital? Well, the quality of your ingredients, or data, directly affects the taste of the final dish, or the performance of your model. Say you're working with a mix of data types, like text categories and numbers. You'll need to convert those text labels into a numerical format that your neural network can digest. Or maybe you're dealing with images. In that case, you might need to adjust the size of the images or even play around with them—like rotating or flipping—to give your model a more varied diet. The goal here is to make sure the data you feed into your neural network is as clean, consistent, and useful as possible. Doing this can make your model's "learning" process much smoother. For example, scaling your data so that all the features are in a similar range can help your model get to the answer more quickly, kind of like how preheating an oven speeds up cooking time. But it's not just about speed; it's also about quality. Proper preprocessing can help your model pick up on the finer details and nuances in the data, making it more accurate in the long run. On the flip side, if you skip this step or do it haphazardly, you're setting yourself up for a longer, more frustrating training process, and you might end up with a model that's not as effective as it could be.

So, if you're diving into neural networks, understanding how to properly preprocess your data isn't just a nice-to-have skill; it's a must-have. Think of it as the secret sauce that can make or break your model's performance. Just like in cooking, good prep work sets the stage for a successful final product.

Practical Steps for Preprocessing the MNIST Dataset

Normalizing the Image Data

Firstly, let's normalize the image data. The pixel values in the MNIST dataset range from 0 to 255. Neural networks often perform better on normalized data, so we'll scale these pixel values down to a range of 0 to 1. You can achieve this by dividing the entire dataset by 255:

```
train_images = train_images.astype("float32") / 255.0
test_images = test_images.astype("float32") / 255.0
```

Here, we first convert the data type of the image arrays to float32. This is necessary because the original dataset is of integer type, and integer division would result in truncated values. We then divide all the pixel values by 255 to normalize them.

Reshaping the Image Data

The MNIST images are grayscale and stored in arrays of shape (28, 28). Depending on the neural network architecture you intend to use, you may need to reshape these arrays. For instance, convolutional neural networks (CNNs) often expect input images to have three dimensions (height, width, channels). Since the MNIST images are grayscale, they have only one channel. To reshape the arrays, you can use:

```
train_images = train_images.reshape(-1, 28, 28, 1)
test_images = test_images.reshape(-1, 28, 28, 1)
```

This reshapes each image to have dimensions (28, 28, 1), indicating height, width, and the number of color channels, respectively.

Encoding the Labels

The MNIST dataset contains labels ranging from 0 to 9, representing the digits in the images. These labels are already in a numerical format, so we don't need to perform any complex transformations like one-hot encoding. However, if you're using a neural network architecture that expects one-hot encoded labels, you can easily convert them using Keras utilities:

```
train_labels = tf.keras.utils.to_categorical(train_labels, 10)
test_labels = tf.keras.utils.to_categorical(test_labels, 10)
```

Here, 10 refers to the number of classes, which are the digits from 0 to 9.

The above MNIST dataset, widely used yet intricate enough for meaningful neural network tasks, requires particular preprocessing steps such as normalization, reshaping, and label encoding to make it compatible with different neural network architectures. These steps not only simplify the dataset but also optimize it for better performance and faster convergence during the training process. With the data now preprocessed, you're set to move on to the next phase of building and training your neural network model.

Introduction to Neural Network Models

What is a Neural Network Model?

Imagine a neural network as a virtual brain built to spot patterns in information. Just like our brains are made of neurons connected by tiny bridges called synapses, a neural network is made of artificial neurons, or "nodes," linked together. These nodes are stacked in layers, and the strength of the connections between them is determined by something called "weights." Think of these weights like friendship levels; the stronger the weight, the more influence one node has on another. The goal is to tweak these weights so that the network's guesses get closer and closer to the right answer. This tweaking process is like a training regimen for the network, helping it get better at tasks ranging from understanding human language to helping self-driving cars navigate.

What makes neural networks so awesome is their flexibility. They're like all-terrain vehicles of the data world. Whether you're dealing with messy stuff like pictures or text, or more organized data like you'd find in a spreadsheet, neural networks can handle it. They learn the hidden patterns in any type of data, making them the go-to tool in the toolbox of machine learning and artificial intelligence. And they can be as simple or as complicated as you need them to be. For straightforward jobs, a "shallow" network with fewer layers will do. But when you're tackling big challenges like understanding human speech or identifying objects in photos, you'll want a "deep" network with many layers, each adding its own level of complexity and understanding.

Architecture of a Neural Network

Basic Components and Structure

The architecture of a simple neural network typically consists of three main types of layers: the input layer, hidden layers, and the output layer. The input layer receives the initial data that the network will learn from and usually has as many neurons as there are features in the data. Hidden layers are where the actual computation happens; they take the inputs, apply a set of functions defined by the model's parameters, and pass the results to the next layer. Finally, the output layer produces the prediction or classification that the model is designed to make.

Role of Activation Functions

Each neuron in a neural network is associated with an activation function, which determines the output of the neuron given a set of inputs. Activation functions introduce non-linearity into the system, allowing the network to learn from the error and make adjustments. Common activation functions include the ReLU (Rectified Linear Unit), Sigmoid, and Tanh. For example, ReLU is defined as f(x)=max(0,x) and is widely used in convolutional neural networks and deep learning models because it helps the network learn faster and perform better.

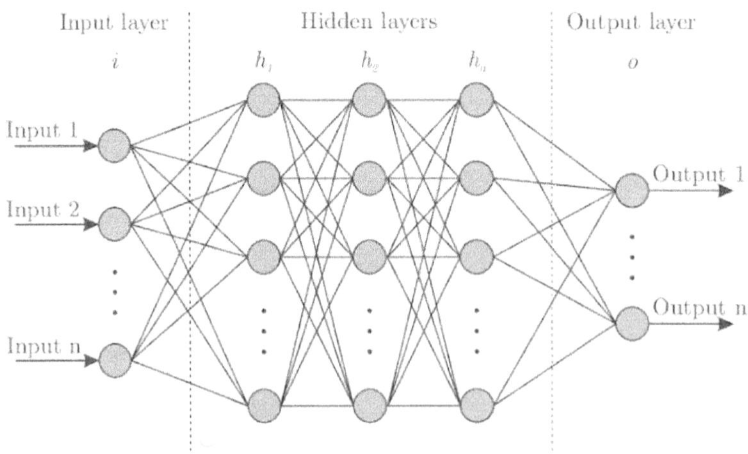

Fig 1.2 Neural Network Architecture

Importance of Weights and Biases

Weights and biases are the learnable parameters in a neural network. Weights control the signal (or the strength of the connection) between two neurons, while biases allow neurons to have some flexibility in activation. During the training process, the network adjusts these weights and biases to minimize the error in its predictions. The values are initialized randomly or using techniques like Xavier initialization and are fine-tuned during training using algorithms like Gradient Descent.

Forward and Backpropagation

The learning process in a neural network involves two main phases: forward propagation and backpropagation. During forward propagation, the network makes a prediction based on the input data by passing it through all the layers from the input to the output. The model's prediction is then compared to the actual target, and the difference (or error) is calculated. Backpropagation is the process of updating the model parameters (weights and biases) to minimize this error. The error is propagated backward through the network, starting from the output layer and moving through the hidden layers, adjusting the weights and biases along the way.

Structure of a Keras Model

Anatomy of a Keras Model

In the world of Keras, think of a model as a blueprint for building a house, where each room is a layer with a specific function. The most straightforward blueprint is the Sequential model, which is like a one-story house where you go from one room to the next in a single line. But if you want a more complex multi-story house with staircases and secret passages, you'll need the Keras functional API. Regardless of the complexity, the core idea is the same: a model is your game plan for turning raw data into useful information. Before you start building, you have to finalize your blueprint by specifying things like the materials you'll use (optimizer), the quality checks (loss function), and what you'll keep an eye on during construction (metrics). Once that's done, you're ready to build your house (train your model), inspect it (evaluate it), and finally, live in it (use it for predictions).

Keras is like the LEGO set of deep learning. Whether you're a kid who just wants to snap a few blocks together or an architect planning a complex structure, Keras has got you covered. It takes a lot of the nitty-gritty details of neural network construction and packs them into easy-to-use building blocks.

This makes it a hit among beginners who are just getting their feet wet in deep learning. But don't let its simplicity fool you; it's also robust enough for experts to craft cutting-edge models. This blend of user-friendliness and depth has made Keras a go-to tool for a wide audience, from researchers in academia to pros in the industry.

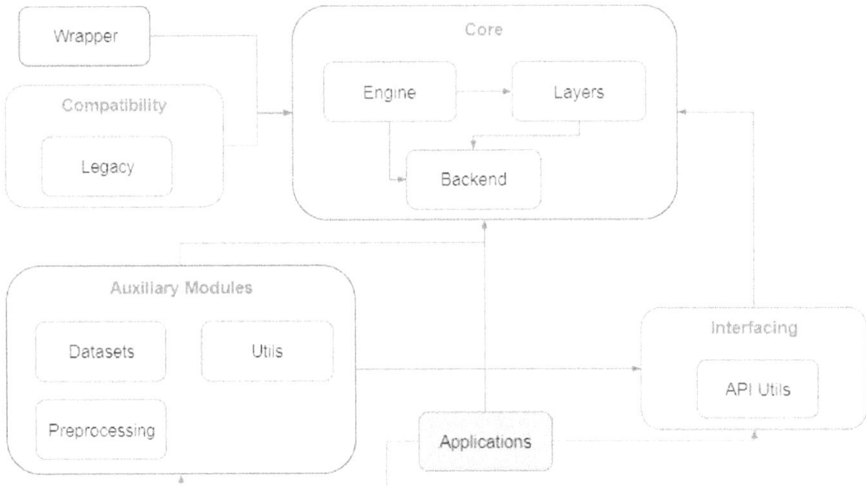

Fig 1.3 Keras Model Structure

Building Keras Model for MNIST

We shall roll up our sleeves and build a simple neural network to sort those handwritten numbers in the MNIST dataset. Imagine this as a single-story house (Sequential model) with just one main room (hidden layer). In Keras, you don't have to lay down the welcome mat (input layer); it figures that out based on the shape of your building materials (training data). For our main room, we'll decorate it with 128 pieces of furniture (neurons) and light it up with ReLU bulbs (activation function). Finally, for the exit (output layer), we'll install 10 doors (neurons), each labeled with a number from 0 to 9, and use a softmax lighting system to show which door is most likely the right choice.

Following is how you'd define this architecture:

```
from tensorflow.keras.models import Sequential
from tensorflow.keras.layers import Flatten, Dense

model = Scquential([
    Flatten(input_shape=(28, 28, 1)),
```

```
    Dense(128, activation='relu'),
    Dense(10, activation='softmax')
])
```

In this code snippet, Flatten takes the 28x28x1 images and flattens them into a 1D array of 784 elements. Dense layers are fully connected layers. The first one has 128 neurons and uses the ReLU activation function. The second Dense layer is the output layer and has 10 neurons for the 10 classes of digits, using softmax as the activation function.

Compilation of the Model

Before training, the model needs to be compiled. During this step, you define the loss function, the optimizer, and other metrics like accuracy. For our model, we'll use the categorical cross-entropy loss, as we're dealing with a multi-class classification problem. The optimizer will be the Adam optimizer, a variant of stochastic gradient descent that has become popular for deep learning.

Following is how to compile the model:

```
model.compile(optimizer='adam',
        loss='categorical_crossentropy',
        metrics=['accuracy'])
```

Keras provides a handy method to view the model's architecture, which can be particularly useful for debugging or for educational purposes. By calling model.summary(), you can see a table that describes each layer, its output shape, and its number of parameters. This is an excellent way to verify that the model looks the way you intended and to get a quick calculation of the total number of trainable parameters.

Summary

In this chapter, we embarked on a foundational journey through the landscape of neural networks, emphasizing practical know-how backed by conceptual understanding. Starting with the importance of a well-configured development environment, we delved into setting up Python, TensorFlow, and Keras on a Linux system. This step-by-step walkthrough aimed to equip you with the necessary tools, setting the stage for efficient and streamlined machine learning projects. The chapter then segued into data handling, introducing the MNIST dataset as a versatile platform for hands-on practice. This dataset of handwritten digits serves as an accessible yet rich resource for multiple neural network architectures, and we walked through the steps to load and preprocess this dataset, preparing it for model training.

We then shifted focus to the core of the chapter, neural networks. Offering an overview of what neural networks are, we learned their architecture, including layers, neurons, activation functions, weights, and biases. Special attention was given to the learning process, involving forward and backpropagation, which allows the network to learn from the data by adjusting its parameters. Subsequently, we explored the architecture of a simple neural network model, providing insights into the role of each component and how they interact during the learning process. This foundational understanding serves as a stepping stone for more complex architectures and applications.

Building on this theoretical groundwork, the chapter culminated in a practical demonstration of constructing a neural network model using Keras. The ease-of-use and flexibility of Keras were highlighted, illustrating how a powerful neural network model could be built with just a few lines of code. For the MNIST dataset, we constructed a simple Sequential model with one hidden layer and an output layer, compiled it, and prepared it for training. This hands-on example encapsulated the essence of the chapter, bridging the gap between theory and practice. Throughout this chapter, the recurring theme has been the seamless integration of conceptual knowledge with practical skills.

CHAPTER 2: DEEP DIVE INTO FEEDFORWARD NETWORKS

Introduction to Feedforward Networks

What Are Feedforward Networks?

Feedforward neural networks are the simplest type of artificial neural network architecture. In these networks, the data moves in one direction—from the input layer, through the hidden layers, to the output layer—without looping back. The term "feedforward" signifies that the connections between the units do not form any cycles, differentiating it from recurrent neural networks where cycles do exist. These are the quintessential networks that most people learn when first venturing into the field of neural networks. They are widely used in pattern recognition tasks, such as handwriting recognition and speech recognition, and serve as the foundational building blocks for more complex types of neural networks.

Applications and Limitations

Feedforward networks excel in tasks where the output is a deterministic function of the input. For example, they are often used in classification problems to map input data to a specific output label. Despite their utility and straightforward architecture, feedforward networks have limitations. They are ill-suited for tasks that involve sequence prediction, time-series analysis, or any application where the current output depends on previous inputs. This is because they lack internal memory to maintain a state between inputs. For such tasks, other architectures like recurrent neural networks or Long Short-Term Memory networks are generally more appropriate.

Architecture of Feedforward Networks

Structure and Layers

Imagine a feedforward neural network as a multi-layered sandwich. The bread slices on either end are the input and output layers, and the fillings in between are the hidden layers. The input layer is like the front door where the data comes in; each "neuron" or node here represents a specific piece of information from your dataset. The hidden layers are the heart of the operation, transforming the data as it passes through. Finally, the output layer is the end of the line, giving you the final answer, whether it's a prediction or a classification. The layers are connected by "weighted links," think of them as highways with tolls that change depending on traffic conditions. These weighted links and special functions in the neurons decide how the data transforms as it moves through the network.

Neurons and Activation Functions

In a feedforward network, each neuron is like a mini-calculator. It takes inputs from all neurons in the layer before it, multiplies them by certain "weights," adds them up, and then pushes them through a special function called an "activation function." This function is the magic wand that adds complexity to the network by allowing it to handle non-linear problems. There are different types of activation functions like Sigmoid, Tanh, and ReLU, and choosing the right one can make or break your network's performance. It's like picking the right seasoning for a dish; the choice depends on what you're cooking.

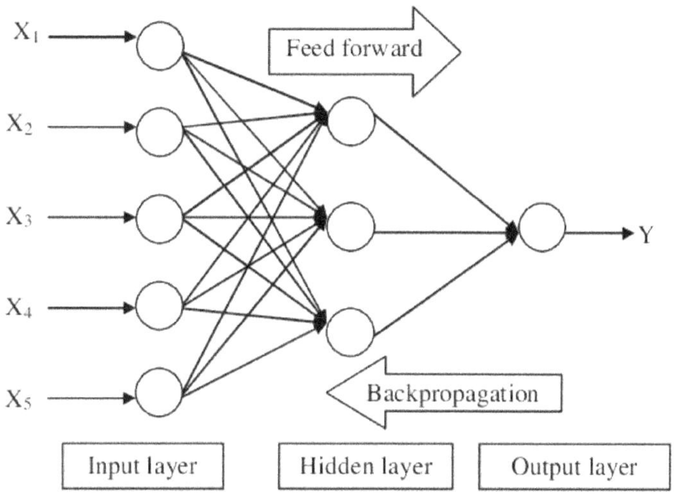

Fig 2.1 Feedforward Network

Importance of Weights

Weights in a feedforward network are like the control knobs on a mixing board. They determine how strong or weak the signal should be as it moves from one neuron to another. During the "training" phase, these weights are fine-tuned to get the network's predictions as close as possible to the real answers. This fine-tuning starts with random settings and uses algorithms like Gradient Descent to iteratively improve them. Each round of adjustments is called a "training epoch." The better these weights are optimized, the smarter your network becomes.

Forward Propagation and Backpropagation

Data in a feedforward network travels in one direction, from the input layer through the hidden layers to the output layer, a process known as "forward propagation." It's like a one-way road trip where the data scenery changes as it passes through different layers. But the journey doesn't end there. There's a return trip called "backpropagation," where the network figures out how far off its predictions were and adjusts the weights accordingly. It's like retracing your steps to find out where you took a wrong turn and correcting your course.

In summary, feedforward neural networks are the foundational building blocks in the realm of neural networks, offering a straightforward yet powerful way to model complex relationships in data. Their architecture consists of an input layer, hidden layers, and an output layer, interconnected by weights that are optimized during training. The activation functions in the neurons introduce the non-linearity that enables the network to learn from errors and make complex decisions.

Activation Functions in Keras

To create a comprehensive and engaging explanation of activation functions in neural networks, we can draw an analogy to a familiar scenario: cooking. Just as the right combination of spices can turn a simple meal into a culinary masterpiece, activation functions are the secret ingredients that give neural networks their power to learn and make sense of complex data.

Magic of Activation Functions

Imagine you're in the kitchen preparing a stew. You have all your main ingredients: meat, vegetables, and broth. But without the right blend of herbs and spices, the stew might taste flat. In the world of neural networks, activation functions are like these spices. They add depth and complexity to the data being processed. Without activation functions, a neural network would be unable to understand the subtle nuances in the data, much like a stew without seasoning can't tantalize your taste buds.

Activation functions bring life to the neural network by allowing it to capture and represent complex patterns. They do this by introducing non-linearity, which is a fancy way of saying they help the network learn from both the straightforward and the intricate, twisty-turny parts of the data. Without non-linearity, a neural network would be as good at learning from data as a blunt knife is at chopping vegetables – not very effective.

Incorporating Activation Functions in Keras

Using activation functions in Keras, a popular deep learning library, is as easy as sprinkling salt into your dish. There are two main ways to add these functions to your neural network, which can be thought of as the layers of your culinary creation. One way is to add them directly into the mix as you're building each layer. For instance, when you're adding a dense layer to your network and you want to use the ReLU activation function, it's as simple as specifying activation='relu' in your code.

The other method is akin to garnishing your finished dish with a sprinkle of fresh herbs. You can add the activation function as a separate layer, which is particularly useful when you want to include additional techniques, like batch normalization, to enhance the learning process. This approach allows you to layer flavors, or in the case of neural networks, layer learning functions for more sophisticated results.

Popular Activation Functions and Their Applications

Just as a master chef knows which spices will best complement the main ingredients of a dish, a skilled data scientist understands how to select the right activation function for a given problem. Keras offers a variety of these functions, each with its own strengths and ideal use cases.

ReLU, or Rectified Linear Unit, is a favorite for its simplicity and effectiveness, particularly when dealing with image data. It's like black pepper – versatile and can be used in almost any dish. Sigmoid and Tanh functions are more like cayenne pepper and paprika; they're perfect for adding a bit of heat to binary classification tasks, where you need a clear yes or no answer. And then there's Softmax, which is like a finishing glaze, bringing together the flavors of a dish. It's used in multi-class classification tasks to highlight the most likely outcome from several possibilities.

Custom Activation Functions and Advanced Features

For those looking to experiment or address specific challenges, Keras offers the ability to define custom activation functions. A custom function can be defined using backend functions provided by Keras, and this custom function can then be used as the activation function for a layer. This feature opens the door for innovative approaches and fine-grained control over the behavior of the network. Keras also supports advanced activation layers like LeakyReLU and Parametric ReLU, which are variations of the standard ReLU function but allow small, non-zero gradients when the input is less than zero, addressing the "dying ReLU" problem where neurons can sometimes get stuck during training.

To wrap it up, activation functions are the unsung heroes of neural networks in Keras. They bring in the much-needed complexity, making your models capable of learning intricate patterns. Whether you're a beginner or an expert, Keras offers a range of options to suit your needs, making it easier than ever to build effective and efficient deep learning models.

Implement Forward Pass with TensorFlow

Preparing Data for Forward Pass

Before we dive into implementing the forward pass, let's briefly touch upon the data preparation. Assuming that you've already preprocessed the MNIST dataset as learned in Chapter 1, you have a 4D tensor representing the training images and a one-hot encoded array for the labels. We've normalized the images and reshaped them to (28, 28, 1). We shall move on to the implementation details.

Building Neural Network Model

We've previously used Keras to build a simple Sequential model for our MNIST dataset. The model included a flatten layer to reshape the input data, followed by a dense hidden layer with 128 neurons and ReLU activation, and finally a dense output layer with 10 neurons and softmax activation. In TensorFlow, this model can be used as is for performing the forward pass. The forward pass is implicitly carried out when you use methods like model.predict() or model.evaluate().

Executing Forward Pass

The actual forward pass in TensorFlow is a straightforward process once your model is built and compiled. To predict the output or probability distribution for a given input, you can use the predict method of the model. Following is how you can do it:

```
# Assuming `test_images` contains a batch of preprocessed images from the MNIST dataset
predicted_output = model.predict(test_images)
```

In the above snippet, predicted_output would contain the softmax probabilities for each class (digits 0-9) for each image in test_images. This is the outcome of the forward pass through the network, starting from the input layer and moving through the hidden layers to the output layer.

Understanding Output

The output of the forward pass is a probability distribution across the 10 classes (digits 0-9 in the case of MNIST). Each row in the output corresponds to an image in the test set, and each column in that row represents the probability that the image belongs to one of the 10 classes. You can convert these probabilities to class labels by taking the index of the maximum value in each row, typically done using TensorFlow's argmax function.

Executing the forward pass is fundamental in neural network operations, serving not only for making predictions but also as the initial step in model training before backpropagation. With the forward pass, we get the model's predictions, which can then be compared to actual labels to compute the loss, serving as the basis for subsequent weight adjustments during backpropagation.

Loss Functions Overview

Role of Loss Functions

Loss functions are a critical part of training neural networks, acting as a scorekeeper for how well the model is performing. They provide a way to measure the difference between the model's predictions and the actual outcomes. This measurement is crucial because it tells us whether the model is on the right track or if it needs to be corrected.

When training a neural network, the goal is to adjust the internal settings so that its predictions get as close to reality as possible. The loss function is the tool that tells us how far off we are. It's like a coach in sports, constantly giving feedback on performance and areas that need improvement.

Types of Loss Functions and Their Applicability

There is a variety of loss functions to choose from, and the choice is often dictated by the type of problem you're trying to solve:

- For regression problems, Mean Squared Error (MSE) is commonly used. In classification problems, Cross-Entropy Loss (also known as Log Loss) is the standard.

- For tasks involving sequence prediction, more advanced loss functions like the Connectionist Temporal Classification (CTC) loss might be used.

- There are even specialized loss functions for generative models, like the Wasserstein loss for Generative Adversarial Networks (GANs).

Each loss function has its mathematical properties that make it more suitable for certain types of problems, and understanding these can be crucial when designing a neural network for a specific task.

Interplay Between Loss Functions and Optimization Algorithms

Once the loss function is defined, an optimization algorithm is used to adjust the model parameters in a way that minimizes the loss. Most optimization algorithms, including popular ones like Gradient Descent and its variants (Stochastic Gradient Descent, Adam, etc.), rely on the concept of a gradient, which is a vector of partial derivatives. The gradient points in the direction of the steepest increase of the loss function. The optimizer uses this information to update the model parameters in the opposite direction, aiming to find the minimum of the loss function. This process is known as backpropagation, where the gradient of the loss function is calculated with respect to each weight by applying the chain rule of calculus.

Loss Functions in Overfitting and Underfitting

An interesting aspect of loss functions is their role in diagnosing issues like overfitting and underfitting, which are common challenges in machine learning. Overfitting occurs when the model learns the training data too well, including its noise and outliers, but fails to generalize to new, unseen data. Underfitting is the opposite; the model is too simple to capture the underlying trend of the data. Monitoring the loss function can provide insights into these issues. A training loss that decreases too quickly and a validation loss that starts to increase is usually a sign of overfitting. If both the training and validation losses are high, the model is likely underfitting.

Loss Functions in Advanced Deep Learning Techniques

In advanced deep learning techniques like transfer learning, multi-task learning, and reinforcement learning, loss functions take on even more nuanced roles. In transfer learning, for instance, you might fine-tune a pre-trained model on a new task using a different loss function that better aligns with the new objectives. In multi-task learning, you could have multiple loss functions, one for each task the model is trained on. In reinforcement learning, the concept of loss is extended to include not just immediate rewards but future rewards as well, often requiring specialized loss functions.

In all these cases, the loss function is key to guiding the training process. It's the measure of success that tells us whether the model is learning what it should be.

Basics of Backpropagation

Significance of Backpropagation in Neural Networks

Backpropagation is a key process in training neural networks. It's like a feedback loop that helps the network learn from its mistakes. After the network makes a guess during the forward pass, backpropagation kicks in to adjust the network's inner settings — the weights and biases — to make better guesses in the future. It's like a self-correction mechanism.

The goal of backpropagation is to reduce errors by finding out which direction will lead to the most significant decrease in the loss function — the measure of the network's inaccuracy. It uses calculus to figure out how to change each weight and bias. This information guides how the network's parameters should be tweaked.

Mechanics of Backpropagation

Following is how it works: after the network makes its predictions, it looks at how wrong those predictions were — that's the loss. Then, starting from the output and moving backward through each layer, it figures out how much each weight contributed to the error. This backward journey is why it's called backpropagation — the error information travels back through the network.

The amount by which the weights are adjusted is controlled by the learning rate. This is a bit like deciding how big of a step to take when you're walking towards a destination. If your steps are too big, you might step right over where you want to go. If they're too small, it could take forever to get there. The learning rate helps you find the right size step to reach the optimal performance without overshooting or taking too long.

Backpropagation in TensorFlow

Automatic Differentiation

One of the strengths of TensorFlow is its automatic differentiation capabilities, which simplify the implementation of backpropagation. TensorFlow's GradientTape API is a powerful tool for this purpose. With GradientTape, you can automatically track operations on trainable variables and then compute gradients with respect to a target (usually a loss) to be minimized. Following is a simplified example using a single batch of data:

```
import tensorflow as tf

# Create some example data and labels
data = tf.constant([[1.0, 2.0], [3.0, 4.0]])
labels = tf.constant([[0.0, 1.0], [1.0, 0.0]])

# Define a simple model
model = tf.keras.Sequential([
    tf.keras.layers.Dense(10, activation='relu'),
    tf.keras.layers.Dense(2, activation='softmax')
])

# Forward pass and loss calculation
with tf.GradientTape() as tape:
    tape.watch(data)
    predictions = model(data)
    loss = tf.keras.losses.categorical_crossentropy(labels, predictions)

# Compute gradients
gradients = tape.gradient(loss, model.trainable_variables)

# Update the weights
```

```
optimizer = tf.keras.optimizers.Adam()
optimizer.apply_gradients(zip(gradients, model.trainable_variables))
```

Understanding Forward Pass to Backpropagation

In the above code snippet, we first define some example data and labels. Then, we create a simple neural network model consisting of a dense layer with 10 neurons and ReLU activation, followed by an output layer with 2 neurons and softmax activation. Inside a tf.GradientTape block, we perform the forward pass by calling model(data) and then compute the loss using the true labels and the model's predictions. The GradientTape keeps track of all operations that occur on trainable variables. After the forward pass, we use tape.gradient() to compute the gradients of the loss concerning each trainable variable. Finally, these gradients are used to update the model's weights using the Adam optimizer.

The beauty of TensorFlow's approach lies in its abstraction. The complexities of the backpropagation algorithm are hidden behind simple and intuitive APIs, making it easy for both beginners and experts to implement complex neural network architectures. However, this abstraction doesn't limit your control over the model. TensorFlow provides various ways to customize the backpropagation process, whether by creating custom loss functions, custom gradients, or even custom training loops. This level of control is particularly useful for research and experimentation, where you might need to deviate from standard practices.

Training Feedforward Model on MNIST

Initializing Model and Data Preparation

We shall start by creating a simple feedforward neural network model using TensorFlow. This model will use the MNIST dataset, which we have already preprocessed and loaded in the development environment. For our feedforward model, we'll employ a simple architecture that includes one hidden layer with 128 neurons and an output layer with 10 neurons corresponding to the digits 0-9. We'll use ReLU as the activation function for the hidden layer and softmax for the output layer.

Defining Model

Following is how to define this feedforward model in TensorFlow:

```
model = tf.keras.Sequential([
  tf.keras.layers.Flatten(input_shape=(28, 28, 1)),
  tf.keras.layers.Dense(128, activation='relu'),
  tf.keras.layers.Dense(10, activation='softmax')
])
```

In the above code, we first flatten the input images from a 28x28 grid into a single vector of 784 elements. Then we add a dense hidden layer with 128 neurons, followed by the output layer with 10 neurons. The ReLU and softmax activation functions are used in the hidden and output layers, respectively.

Compilation and Training

Before training the model, we need to compile it. Compilation involves specifying the optimizer, the loss function, and any additional metrics we want to track during training. For our model, we'll use the Adam optimizer and the categorical cross-entropy loss function, suitable for multi-class classification problems like MNIST.

```
model.compile(optimizer='adam',
        loss='categorical_crossentropy',
        metrics=['accuracy'])
```

To train the model, we use the fit method, which takes the training data, training labels, number of epochs, and batch size as arguments. For this example, let's train the model for 10 epochs using a batch size of 32.

```
model.fit(train_images, train_labels, epochs=10, batch_size=32)
```

Evaluating Model Performance

After training, it's crucial to evaluate the model's performance on a dataset it hasn't seen before. This is generally done using a separate validation or test set. The MNIST dataset usually comes with a predefined test set, which we can use for this purpose.

```
test_loss, test_accuracy = model.evaluate(test_images, test_labels)
```

Here, test_loss and test_accuracy give us a quantitative measure of how well our model is performing. It's good practice to compare these metrics with the training loss and accuracy to ensure that the model is not overfitting or underfitting. Here, we've successfully defined, compiled, and trained a simple feedforward neural network model on the MNIST dataset using TensorFlow. This comprehensive process of building and training a neural network provides a strong and healthy start to dive into more complex architectures and applications.

Explore Regularization Techniques

Need for Regularization

Regularization techniques are essential tools in the arsenal of any machine learning practitioner. As neural networks become deeper and more complex, they become increasingly prone to overfitting the training data, which means they perform exceptionally well on the data they've seen but poorly on new, unseen data. This is where regularization comes into play. It aims to constrain the optimization process, discouraging the model from fitting to the high variance in the training data, thus enabling the model to generalize better to new data.

L1 and L2 Regularization

One of the most straightforward regularization techniques is the addition of a penalty term to the loss function. L1 and L2 regularization are the most commonly used forms of these. L1 regularization adds a term proportional to the absolute value of the weights, while L2 regularization adds a term proportional to the square of the weights. In Keras, you can add these regularization terms directly when defining layers. For example, to add L2 regularization to a dense layer, you would write:

```
from tensorflow.keras import regularizers

model.add(tf.keras.layers.Dense(128, activation='relu',
kernel_regularizer=regularizers.l2(0.01)))
```

Here, 0.01 is the regularization coefficient, determining the strength of the regularization. The higher this value, the more significant the regularization effect.

Dropout

Dropout is another widely used regularization technique that involves randomly setting a fraction of the input units to 0 during training, which helps to prevent overfitting. In Keras, adding dropout to your model is straightforward:

```
model.add(tf.keras.layers.Dropout(0.5))
```

In the above snippet, approximately 50% of the neurons in the previous layer will be "dropped out," or deactivated, during each training iteration. This random deactivation prevents any single neuron from becoming overly specialized, thus contributing to better generalization.

Batch Normalization

Batch normalization is another technique that, while not originally intended as a regularization method, has been found to have a regularizing effect. This method normalizes the activations of the neurons in a given layer across each mini-batch. This normalization helps ameliorate the problems of vanishing or exploding gradients, making the network easier to train and often reducing the need for dropout or other regularization methods. In Keras, batch normalization can be added as follows:

```
model.add(tf.keras.layers.BatchNormalization())
```

Layer and Activity Regularizers

Keras also offers more advanced regularization options, like layer regularizers and activity regularizers. Layer regularizers act on the layer's output, whereas activity regularizers act on the layer's activation. These can be useful for specialized use-cases where the typical regularization methods may not be sufficient.

Introduction to Hyperparameter Tuning

Importance of Hyperparameter Tuning

Hyperparameter tuning stands as an essential phase in the machine learning pipeline, directly influencing the efficacy of a predictive model. Unlike model parameters, which are derived through training, hyperparameters are set before the training commences. These include settings such as the learning rate, the architecture of a neural network (like the number of hidden layers and neurons), the regularization strength, and the batch size during training. The crux of hyperparameter tuning is to identify the optimal set of these configurations that enable the model to deliver the most precise predictions for the task at hand.

The significance of hyperparameter tuning cannot be overstated. It is the process that can elevate a model from mediocre to superior performance. Since hyperparameters are not learned automatically, the responsibility falls on the machine learning practitioner to determine the best values. This process is often iterative and can be quite challenging, but its impact on the model's performance is profound.

Grid Search

One of the most straightforward strategies for hyperparameter tuning is Grid Search. This method involves specifying a subset of the hyperparameter space as a grid and then evaluating all the combinations in this grid. For example, if you have two hyperparameters, and you decide to test them at three different levels, you would end up running 3×3=9 different training runs. While grid search is simple and easy to parallelize, it can be computationally expensive and time-consuming, especially as the number of hyperparameters grows.

Random Search

An alternative to Grid Search is Random Search. This method selects random combinations of hyperparameters to test, allowing for a continuous exploration of the hyperparameter space. Random Search can be more efficient than Grid Search, particularly when dealing with a high number of hyperparameters. The underlying principle is that not all hyperparameters have an equal impact on the model's performance, and Random Search can more rapidly pinpoint the most influential ones.

Bayesian Optimization

Bayesian Optimization represents a more advanced form of hyperparameter tuning. It constructs a probabilistic model that estimates the performance of different hyperparameter combinations and then iteratively selects new hyperparameters to test based on this model. The approach is designed to balance exploration of new hyperparameters against the exploitation of those that have already shown promise. Bayesian Optimization is especially advantageous when evaluations of the model are costly, which is often the case with complex deep learning models.

Automated Machine Learning (AutoML)

At the forefront of hyperparameter tuning is Automated Machine Learning (AutoML), which automates the selection of both the optimal hyperparameters and the most suitable machine learning algorithms for a given problem. AutoML solutions, such as Google's AutoML and H2O.ai, employ a variety of advanced strategies, including meta-learning and ensemble methods, to optimize performance. While AutoML can deliver impressive results, it typically demands significant computational power. The choice among these methods depends on several factors, including computational budget, model complexity, and the size of the hyperparameter space.

Summary

In this chapter, we delved into the intricacies of training a neural network, focusing on a feedforward model trained on the MNIST dataset. We covered the entire lifecycle of a neural network model, from initializing and defining the architecture to compiling and training it. The chapter emphasized the importance of choosing the right optimizer and loss function during the compilation stage, and how these choices are crucial for the successful training of the model. We also demonstrated how to evaluate the model's performance using a separate test set, providing quantitative metrics that indicate the model's readiness for deployment or the need for further tuning.

Regularization techniques were introduced as a solution to the common problem of overfitting in neural networks. Various strategies like L1 and L2 regularization, Dropout, and Batch Normalization were learned. Each of these techniques adds a unique flavor of complexity to the model, aiming to prevent overfitting and improve generalization to new, unseen data. These methods offer a balance between model complexity and the ability to generalize, serving as essential tools for building robust neural network models.

Hyperparameter tuning was another significant focus, offering methods to optimize the model's performance further. The chapter presented various strategies for hyperparameter tuning, including Grid Search, Random Search, Bayesian Optimization, and Automated Machine Learning (AutoML). Each method has its advantages and drawbacks, offering different trade-offs between computational complexity and optimization effectiveness. The choice of hyperparameter tuning method often depends on various factors like computational resources, model complexity, and the specific needs of the project.

The chapter provided a comprehensive understanding of neural network training, emphasizing practical aspects. It equipped you with the knowledge and tools to not only build and train a neural network model but also to fine-tune it for optimal performance. This information serves as a foundation for exploring more complex neural network architectures and training strategies in subsequent chapters.

Chapter 3: Convolutional Networks for Visual Tasks

Explore Convolutional Layers

Convolutional Layers in Image Processing

Convolutional layers are the building blocks of Convolutional Neural Networks (CNNs), which are widely used in processing images and other data with a grid-like structure. These layers utilize a mathematical process called convolution, which is pivotal for computer vision tasks such as image recognition and object detection. The convolution involves a filter or kernel, which is a small matrix that moves across the input image to produce a feature map. This map is a transformed version of the input that highlights certain features, making it easier for the network to process.

Convolution Operations - Filters and Feature Maps

In practice, a convolutional layer doesn't just have one filter; it has several, each designed to detect different features in the image, such as edges, textures, or more complex patterns. As these filters scan the image, they create a set of feature maps that represent where in the image those features are found. These maps are then stacked together to form the output of the layer, which is passed on to the next layer in the network. This allows the network to build a complex understanding of the image by focusing on different aspects at each layer.

Stride and Padding in Convolutional Layers

The operation of convolutional layers is fine-tuned by two key parameters: stride and padding. The stride determines how far the filter moves across the image each time it makes a pass. A smaller stride means the filter moves in smaller steps, which can capture more detail but requires more computation. Padding is about adding a layer of zeros around the image so that the filter can cover the edge areas without reducing the size of the feature maps. This is especially important in tasks where the precise location of features is crucial, such as in object detection or segmenting images into different regions.

Activation Functions in Convolutional Layers

After the convolution operation, an activation function is usually applied to introduce non-linearity into the system. The ReLU (Rectified Linear Unit) activation function is commonly used in convolutional layers. The purpose of this non-linearity is to enable the network to learn from the error and make adjustments, which is crucial for the learning process. While other activation functions like sigmoid or tanh can also be used, ReLU is often preferred due to its computational efficiency and effectiveness in enabling deep networks to learn from backpropagated errors.

Pooling Layers

Although not a type of convolutional layer, pooling layers often accompany them in CNN architectures. Pooling layers reduce the spatial dimensions (width & height) of the input volume and are used between successive convolutional layers. The most common type is max-pooling, which propagates only the maximum value from a subsection of the feature map to the next layer. This operation serves to reduce the computational complexity and to provide a form of translational invariance, making the network more robust to variations in the input.

The careful tuning of hyperparameters like stride and padding, the strategic use of activation functions, and the integration of pooling layers all contribute to the powerful capabilities of CNNs in image processing and analysis. This intricate dance of operations within convolutional layers is what allows neural networks to achieve remarkable performance in tasks that require a deep understanding of visual data.

Design Convolutional Neural Network (CNN)

CNN Architecture

When architecting a Convolutional Neural Network, it's essential to consider the specific problem you're trying to solve. The architecture varies based on whether you're dealing with image classification, object detection, semantic segmentation, or other advanced vision tasks. However, the core concept remains the same: start with convolutional layers to capture local features, followed by pooling layers to reduce dimensionality, and finally, add fully connected layers for classification or other tasks.

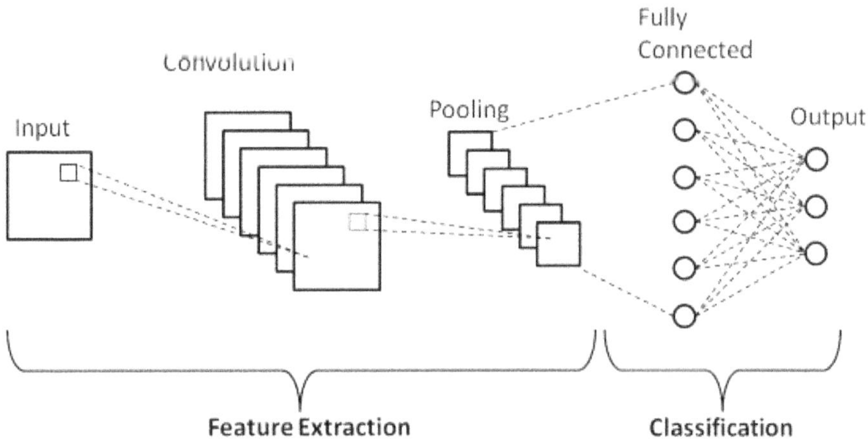

Fig 3.1 CNN Architecture Explained

One of the key ideas behind CNNs is hierarchical feature learning. Initial layers typically capture basic attributes like edges and corners. As you go deeper into the network, the layers focus on increasingly abstract features. For example, a layer deep in the network might specialize in identifying features like a dog's snout or eyes. This natural progression of abstraction is what makes CNNs so powerful for image-related tasks.

While not strictly convolutional layers, pooling layers are an integral part of most CNN architectures. By reducing the spatial dimensions of the feature maps, pooling layers contribute to the model's translational invariance and decrease computational complexity. This enables the model to focus on the essential features and makes it less sensitive to variations and distortions in the input images.

Towards the end of the architecture, you usually find one or more fully connected layers. These layers take the high-level features identified by the preceding convolutional layers and perform tasks like classification. The final layer generally has as many neurons as there are classes in the classification problem, with activation functions like softmax to provide probabilities for each class.

Sample Program: Designing Multi-layer CNN

Embarking on the practical journey of designing a multi-layer Convolutional Neural Network (CNN) using TensorFlow and Keras can be an exciting venture. Imagine we are faced with the challenge of classifying images into one of ten distinct categories. This task is a common starting point for many machine learning enthusiasts and professionals alike, as it encapsulates the fundamental principles of image classification while also introducing the complexities of working with multi-layer networks.

To construct such a network, we would begin by defining the architecture in TensorFlow with the help of Keras:

```
# Initialize the model
cnn_model = tf.keras.Sequential()

# First Convolutional Layer: 32 filters, 3x3 kernel, ReLU activation
cnn_model.add(tf.keras.layers.Conv2D(32, (3, 3), activation='relu', input_shape=(28, 28, 1)))

# First Pooling Layer: Max-pooling with 2x2 grid
cnn_model.add(tf.keras.layers.MaxPooling2D((2, 2)))

# Second Convolutional Layer: 64 filters, 3x3 kernel, ReLU activation
cnn_model.add(tf.keras.layers.Conv2D(64, (3, 3), activation='relu'))

# Second Pooling Layer: Max-pooling with 2x2 grid
cnn_model.add(tf.keras.layers.MaxPooling2D((2, 2)))

# Third Convolutional Layer: 128 filters, 3x3 kernel, ReLU activation
cnn_model.add(tf.keras.layers.Conv2D(128, (3, 3), activation='relu'))

# Flattening: Flatten the 3D output to 1D tensor
cnn_model.add(tf.keras.layers.Flatten())

# Fully Connected Layer: 128 neurons, ReLU activation
cnn_model.add(tf.keras.layers.Dense(128, activation='relu'))

# Output Layer: 10 neurons (one for each category), Softmax activation
cnn_model.add(tf.keras.layers.Dense(10, activation='softmax'))
```

```
# Compile the model
cnn_model.compile(optimizer='adam', loss='categorical_crossentropy', metrics=['accuracy'])
```

In the above program, the CNN architecture starts with an initial convolutional layer using 32 filters and a 3x3 kernel size, followed by a max-pooling layer. The second and third convolutional layers use 64 and 128 filters, respectively, each followed by another max-pooling layer. As you can see, the number of filters increases with each subsequent layer, allowing the network to capture more complex features. After the convolutional layers, we flatten the output and pass it through a fully connected layer with 128 neurons, which then connects to the final output layer with 10 neurons, corresponding to the ten categories we aim to classify.

Once the architecture is defined, the next step is to compile the model, specifying the optimizer, loss function, and metrics to monitor. The model is then ready to be trained on your dataset using the fit method.

Designing a CNN is a blend of choosing the right components and setting them up in a sequence that captures the hierarchical features present in the data, allowing the model to generalize well to new, unseen data. The power of CNNs lies in their ability to automatically and adaptively learn spatial hierarchies of features, and thereafter image classification tasks.

Pooling and Normalization Techniques

Understanding Pooling Layers

Pooling layers serve as a down-sampling mechanism in Convolutional Neural Networks, typically placed between successive convolutional layers. The primary purpose of pooling is to reduce the spatial dimensions of the feature maps, thereby reducing the number of parameters and computations in the network. This dimensionality reduction is crucial for creating a more manageable and generalized model. While the convolutional layers are responsible for feature detection, pooling layers consolidate these features, making the model more robust and less sensitive to variations and distortions in the input images. The most commonly used pooling technique is max-pooling, where the maximum value from a small grid in the feature map is taken as the representative value for that region. This approach has the advantage of being both computationally efficient and effective in retaining important features.

Essence of Normalization Techniques

Normalization in neural networks aims to standardize the inputs or outputs for each layer, stabilizing and accelerating the training process. While normalization techniques can be applied to the inputs of the network, they are often integrated into the architecture itself. One of the most popular normalization techniques is Batch Normalization. This technique normalizes the activations of each layer so that they maintain a mean output activation close to zero and standard deviation close to one. It acts as a regularizer, reducing the risk of overfitting, and often eliminates the need for Dropout layers. Batch Normalization ensures that each layer in a deep network has a roughly consistent distribution of inputs and gradients, making the training process more stable and faster.

In practice, pooling and normalization layers are strategically placed within the CNN architecture to optimize performance. For instance, a pooling layer is commonly added after one or more convolutional layers to reduce dimensionality. Similarly, Batch Normalization layers are often inserted after convolutional layers and before activation functions. Their placement is not arbitrary but is rather determined by the specific requirements of the network and the problem it aims to solve.

Implementing Pooling and Normalization

We shall revisit the CNN architecture we designed earlier and integrate pooling and normalization layers into it. Below is the modified code, now incorporating max-pooling and Batch Normalization:

```
# Initialize the model
modified_cnn_model = tf.keras.Sequential()

# First Convolutional Layer followed by Batch Normalization and Max-Pooling
modified_cnn_model.add(tf.keras.layers.Conv2D(32, (3, 3), activation='relu', input_shape=(28, 28, 1)))
modified_cnn_model.add(tf.keras.layers.BatchNormalization())
modified_cnn_model.add(tf.keras.layers.MaxPooling2D((2, 2)))

# Second Convolutional Layer followed by Batch Normalization and Max-Pooling
modified_cnn_model.add(tf.keras.layers.Conv2D(64, (3, 3), activation='relu'))
```

```
modified_cnn_model.add(tf.keras.layers.BatchNormalization())
modified_cnn_model.add(tf.keras.layers.MaxPooling2D((2, 2)))

# Third Convolutional Layer followed by Batch Normalization
modified_cnn_model.add(tf.keras.layers.Conv2D(128, (3, 3), activation='relu'))
modified_cnn_model.add(tf.keras.layers.BatchNormalization())

# Flattening the output and Fully Connected Layers
modified_cnn_model.add(tf.keras.layers.Flatten())
modified_cnn_model.add(tf.keras.layers.Dense(128, activation='relu'))
modified_cnn_model.add(tf.keras.layers.BatchNormalization())
modified_cnn_model.add(tf.keras.layers.Dense(10, activation='softmax'))

# Compile the model
modified_cnn_model.compile(optimizer='adam', loss='categorical_crossentropy',
metrics=['accuracy'])
```

In the modified architecture, Batch Normalization layers are added right after each convolutional layer and before the activation functions. These layers will normalize the activations, making sure they don't reach extremely high or low values, which can be detrimental to the learning process. Also, max-pooling layers are still present after the first and second convolutional layers, serving their role in down-sampling the feature maps.

Pooling and normalization layers are not just supplementary but rather fundamental aspects of a well-functioning CNN. They play vital roles in reducing computational complexity, improving training stability, and enhancing the model's generalization capabilities. By thoughtfully integrating these layers into a CNN architecture, we can build more robust and efficient models capable of tackling complex image-related tasks. Their significance becomes even more apparent in larger and deeper networks where the risks of overfitting and unstable training are much higher. Therefore, understanding and effectively utilizing these techniques are crucial for anyone working in the field of deep learning and computer vision.

Training Strategies for CNN Models

Data Augmentation

One of the most commonly employed training strategies for CNNs is data augmentation. Given that large datasets are not always available, data augmentation artificially increases the size of the training set by applying various transformations to the input images, such as rotation, flipping, zooming, and shifting. This technique not only provides more data for the model to learn from but also helps improve the model's ability to generalize to new, unseen data. Data augmentation is particularly useful in scenarios where the dataset is imbalanced or when overfitting is a concern.

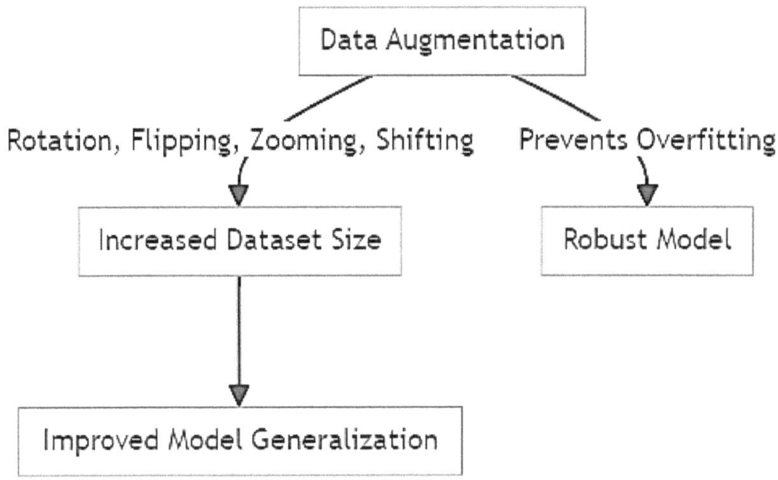

Fig 3.2 Data Augmentation Overview

By introducing variability in the training data, the model becomes more robust and less likely to memorize the training set, thereby improving its performance on the validation or test sets.

Early Stopping and Model Checkpointing

Early stopping is another effective strategy to prevent overfitting. During the training process, the model's performance is monitored on a validation set. If the model's performance starts to degrade (i.e., the validation loss starts increasing while the training loss continues to decrease), the training is halted. This ensures that the model doesn't overfit the training data.

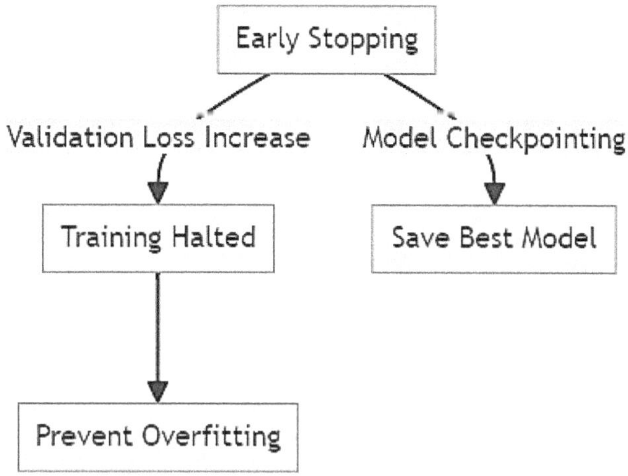

Fig 3.3 Early Stopping Overview

In conjunction with early stopping, model checkpointing can be used to save the model at its best-performing epoch, allowing you to revert to the most effective version of your model. These techniques often go hand-in-hand and are especially beneficial when training deep and complex CNN architectures.

Transfer Learning for Efficient Training

Transfer learning is another powerful strategy, especially when you have limited data. In this approach, a pre-trained model, often trained on a large dataset like ImageNet, is used as a starting point. Depending on the task, you can choose to fine-tune some or all of the layers of the pre-trained model.

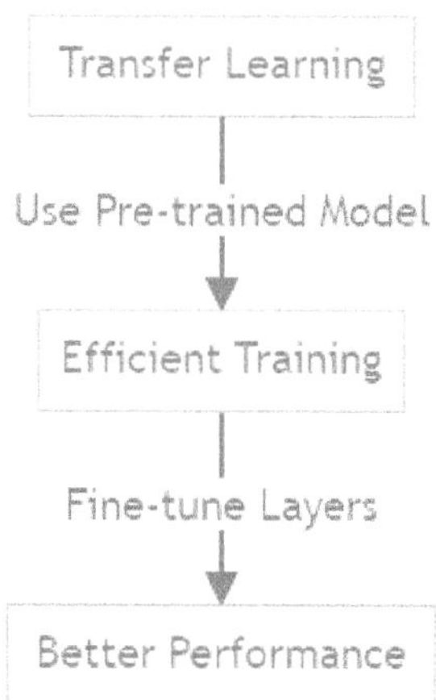

Fig 3.4 Transfer Learning Overview

This not only speeds up the training process but often results in better performance since the model has already learned useful features from the large dataset it was initially trained on. Transfer learning is particularly beneficial for tasks that are similar to the one the pre-trained model was trained for, allowing you to leverage the learned features effectively.

Adaptive Learning Rate Methods

Learning rate plays a crucial role in the training of CNNs. Methods like AdaGrad, RMSprop, and Adam adjust the learning rate during training, either for each parameter or for groups of parameters. These adaptive learning rate methods can lead to faster convergence and can also improve the final performance of the model. The Adam optimizer, for instance, combines the advantages of both AdaGrad and RMSprop, and is often the go-to optimizer for many deep learning tasks.

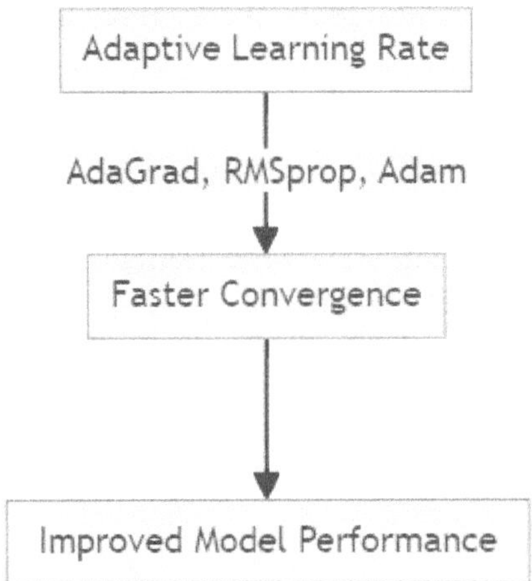

Fig 3.5 Adaptive Learning Rate Overview

Sample Program: Applying Data Augmentation

We shall take our previously designed multi-layer CNN model and apply the data augmentation strategy for training. We'll use TensorFlow's ImageDataGenerator to perform real-time data augmentation.

```
from tensorflow.keras.preprocessing.image import ImageDataGenerator
```

```
# Create an ImageDataGenerator object for data augmentation
datagen = ImageDataGenerator(
    rotation_range=20,
    width_shift_range=0.2,
    height_shift_range=0.2,
    horizontal_flip=True
)

# Prepare the generator
datagen.fit(train_images)

# Train the model using data augmentation
history = modified_cnn_model.fit(
    datagen.flow(train_images, train_labels, batch_size=32),
    steps_per_epoch=len(train_images) / 32,
    epochs=20,
    validation_data=(val_images, val_labels),
    callbacks=[tf.keras.callbacks.EarlyStopping(monitor='val_loss', patience=3)]
)
```

In the above program, we first create an ImageDataGenerator object and configure it to perform various data augmentation techniques like rotation, width and height shifting, and horizontal flipping. We then fit this generator to our training images. During training, the model will receive batches of augmented images, thereby effectively increasing the size and variability of the training set. The Early Stopping callback is also used to monitor the validation loss and stop the training process if the model starts to overfit.

Training a CNN involves much more than just feeding data through a network and backpropagating the errors. It's a meticulous process that requires a thoughtful combination of various strategies and techniques. These strategies not only aim to improve the model's performance but also seek to make the training process more efficient and robust. Whether it's data augmentation for better generalization, early stopping for preventing overfitting, transfer learning for leveraging pre-trained models, or adaptive learning rates for faster convergence—each strategy has its unique role and significance. Understanding how and when to apply these strategies can make the difference between an average model and a highly effective one.

Summary

This chapter provided a comprehensive look at Convolutional Neural Networks (CNNs), diving deep into their architecture, the roles of different layers, and essential training strategies. Starting with the foundational convolutional layers, the chapter elucidated how these layers are designed to capture hierarchical features in images, progressing from basic elements like edges to more complex structures. Pooling and normalization techniques were learned as crucial components that enhance the network's efficiency and robustness. The implementation of these layers was practically demonstrated, enriching the initial multi-layer CNN architecture with added functionality and optimization.

Training strategies emerged as a focal point, emphasizing the importance of methods beyond the basic backpropagation algorithm. Techniques like data augmentation, early stopping, and adaptive learning rates were covered, each contributing uniquely to the model's performance and training efficiency. A hands-on example showcased the application of data augmentation using TensorFlow's ImageDataGenerator, which serves to increase the training set's size and diversity, ultimately leading to a more robust model.

The chapter managed to bridge the conceptual and practical aspects of CNNs seamlessly, equipping you with the knowledge and tools to build, optimize, and train robust models for complex image-related tasks. By the end, you are well-prepared to engage with more advanced CNN architectures and training approaches, a necessary step for anyone aspiring to master the domain of computer vision and deep learning.

Chapter 4: Recurrent Networks for Sequence Data

Introduction to Recurrent Neural Networks

Recurrent Neural Networks (RNNs) stand apart from other neural network architectures due to their ability to process sequences of data, making them particularly well-suited for tasks like time series analysis, natural language processing, and video recognition. Unlike traditional neural networks, which assume independence between inputs, RNNs are designed to recognize patterns across time-steps. This sequence-awareness is achieved by looping the network's output back into itself, allowing information to persist. In essence, an RNN has a "memory" that captures information about previous steps in the sequence, providing a form of internal contextual state that influences future predictions or decisions.

Basic Architecture of an RNN

At its core, an RNN consists of a simple architecture with three main layers: the input layer, a hidden recurrent layer, and the output layer. The hidden layer is where the magic happens; it not only receives input from the data but also gets its previous state as an additional input. This recurrent loop allows the hidden layer to maintain a state across the sequence. Each time-step in the sequence runs through the network, which updates its state based on both the new input and the previous state. This mechanism gives RNNs the ability to capture temporal dependencies in the data.

A key aspect to understanding RNNs is the concept of time-steps. When an RNN processes a sequence, each element in the sequence is considered one "time-step." For example, in natural language processing, each word in a sentence could be one time-step. The RNN processes these time-steps sequentially, updating its state at each step. This is often visualized by "unfolding" the RNN through time, where each time-step is represented as a separate layer in the unfolded network. The same set of weights is used at each time-step, emphasizing the recurrent nature of the network.

Vanishing and Exploding Gradients

While RNNs offer remarkable capabilities for sequence modeling, they are not without limitations. One of the most prominent challenges is the vanishing and exploding gradient problem, which occurs during backpropagation through time (BPTT). In long sequences, the gradients can either become too small (vanish) or too large (explode), making the network difficult to train. This issue has led to the development of more advanced RNN architectures like Long Short-Term Memory (LSTM) and Gated Recurrent Unit (GRU) networks, which are designed to capture long-term dependencies more effectively.

LSTM and GRU

As a response to the limitations of basic RNNs, Long Short-Term Memory (LSTM) networks and Gated Recurrent Unit (GRU) networks were developed. These architectures incorporate gating mechanisms that control the flow of information through the network. LSTMs, for instance, have a complex cell structure with input, output, and forget gates that regulate what information is stored, discarded, or passed on to the next time-step. GRUs are a simplified version of LSTMs, offering similar performance but with fewer parameters, making them more computationally efficient. These advanced RNN variants have proven to be highly effective in tasks that require modeling of long-term dependencies, significantly mitigating the issues of vanishing and exploding gradients.

While they excel in sequence-dependent tasks, basic RNNs are limited by issues related to long-term dependency learning, paving the way for advanced architectures like LSTMs and GRUs. Understanding the intricacies of RNN architecture is crucial for anyone aiming to delve into sequence modeling and time-dependent data analysis.

Vanilla RNNs using Keras

Before diving into code, it's crucial to conceptualize what a Vanilla RNN, also known simply as a basic RNN, looks like in practice. In Keras, constructing an RNN is remarkably straightforward thanks to the high-level APIs that the library provides. When you're building an RNN using Keras, you're fundamentally stacking layers just as you would in a feedforward neural network, but with a twist: you're using recurrent layers that maintain a hidden state across time-steps. For our example, let's consider a simple task of sequence prediction, which could be extended to applications like time-series forecasting or even natural language processing tasks like text generation.

Key Steps for RNNs

To build an RNN in Keras, you'll essentially go through a series of steps:

1. Define the architecture by initializing a Sequential model and then adding the RNN layers.
2. Compile the model by specifying the loss function and the optimizer.
3. Fit the model to the training data.

Code Snippet for Vanilla RNN

Following is a simple example that outlines how to build a basic RNN for sequence prediction using Keras:

```
from tensorflow.keras.models import Sequential
from tensorflow.keras.layers import SimpleRNN, Dense

# Initialize the Sequential model
model = Sequential()

# Add a SimpleRNN layer with 50 units, input shape (None, 10), and return_sequences=True
model.add(SimpleRNN(50, input_shape=(None, 10), return_sequences=True))

# Add another SimpleRNN layer with 50 units
model.add(SimpleRNN(50))

# Add a Dense output layer with 1 unit (for regression)
model.add(Dense(1))

# Compile the model
model.compile(optimizer='adam', loss='mean_squared_error')

# Summary to display architecture
model.summary()
```

In this code snippet, we first import the necessary modules from Keras. We then initialize a Sequential model and add a SimpleRNN layer with 50 hidden units. The input_shape parameter specifies the shape of the input data, where we expect sequences of undefined length (None) and 10 features. The return_sequences=True argument is crucial when stacking RNN layers so that the subsequent RNN layer receives sequences and not just the output of the last time-step. After the recurrent layers, we add a final Dense layer with a single output unit, suitable for regression tasks.

Compiling and Training the Model

After defining the architecture, the next step is to compile the model. In the above program, we use the Adam optimizer and the Mean Squared Error loss function, which is commonly used for regression tasks. The model.compile() method takes care of this, and you are then ready to fit your model to the training data using model.fit(). Training a Vanilla RNN is similar to training any other neural network in Keras; however, ensure that your input data shape matches the input_shape specified in the first recurrent layer.

Significance and Limitations of Vanilla RNNs

While Vanilla RNNs are the simplest form of recurrent neural networks, they serve as a foundational building block for understanding more complex architectures like LSTMs and GRUs. They are excellent for learning short-term dependencies but struggle with long-term dependencies due to the vanishing gradient problem. Despite this limitation, understanding how to construct and train a Vanilla RNN is a critical skill. It offers a stepping stone to grasp the mechanics of recurrent layers and sets the stage for diving into more advanced RNN architectures.

Overall, building a Vanilla RNN in Keras involves defining a sequential model, adding SimpleRNN layers for the recurrent part, and compiling the model with an appropriate optimizer and loss function. This provides a practical entry point into the world of sequence modeling, serving as a foundational step for more complex tasks and architectures.

Long Short-Term Memory (LSTM) Networks

While Vanilla RNNs provide a good starting point for sequence modeling, they come with limitations, particularly when it comes to learning long-term dependencies. In long sequences, the gradients computed during backpropagation can either vanish or explode, making the network difficult to train effectively. This is where Long Short-Term Memory (LSTM) networks come into play. Developed by Hochreiter and Schmidhuber in 1997, LSTMs are designed to combat the vanishing gradient problem, allowing for more effective training of deep networks on sequence tasks that require understanding over long durations.

Core Architecture of LSTMs

LSTMs introduce a more complex internal structure compared to Vanilla RNNs. While the basic RNN has a simple loop that connects the hidden layer across time-steps, LSTMs have a specially designed cell state that runs horizontally across all time-steps, in addition to the hidden state. This cell state serves as a "highway," allowing gradients to flow more easily from one end of the sequence to the other. The cell state is modulated by various gates: the input gate, the forget gate, and the output gate. These gates determine what information gets added or removed as the cell state gets passed along the sequence.

The gates are essentially small neural networks with sigmoid activations, outputting values between 0 and 1 to decide the amount of information to pass through. The input gate decides what new information will be stored in the cell state. The forget gate determines what portions of the cell state should be thrown away or kept. Finally, the output gate decides what parts of the cell state make it to the hidden state, which is then passed to the next layer or becomes the final output. Through these mechanisms, LSTMs can learn which information is relevant to keep or discard for making predictions, thereby capturing long-term dependencies effectively.

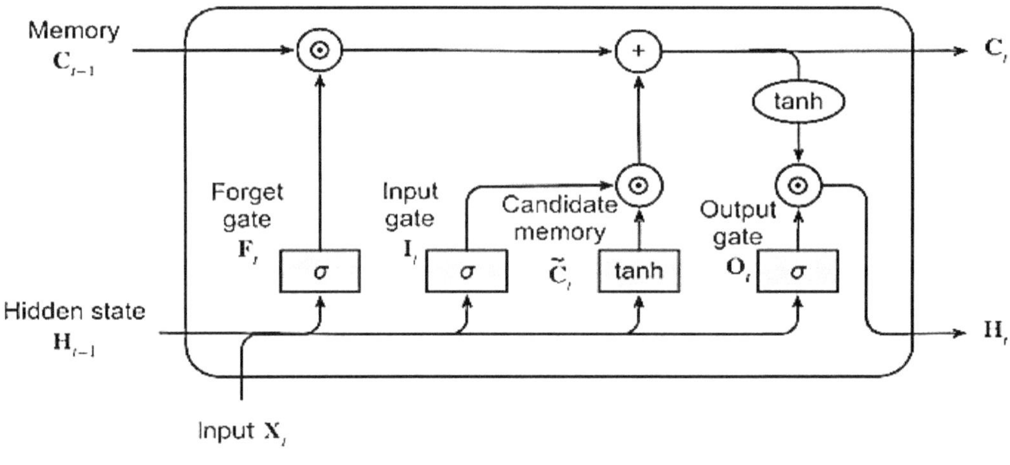

Fig 4.1 LSTM Architecture

The LSTM's Internal Process

The LSTM cell makes decisions about what to store, discard, and output via the gates at each time step. Following is a step-by-step breakdown of the processes within an LSTM cell:

1. Deciding What to Forget: The forget gate takes the previous hidden state and the current input, applies a sigmoid function, and decides which parts of the cell state to let through.

2. Deciding What to Store: The input gate uses a sigmoid layer to decide which values it will update and a tanh layer to create a vector of new candidate values. It then combines these two to update the cell state.

3. Updating the Cell State: The old cell state is updated into the new cell state. The forgotten information is discarded, and the new candidate values, scaled by how much they were decided to be updated, are added.

4. Deciding What to Output: Finally, the output gate decides what the next hidden state should be. The cell state is put through a tanh function (to push the values to be between -1 and 1) and then multiplied by the output of the sigmoid gate, so that only the parts of the cell state that are decided to be output are actually produced.

There are several variants of LSTMs that include additional or altered gates for different purposes. For example, Gated Recurrent Units (GRUs) are a variant of LSTMs that combine the forget and input gates into a single "update gate" and merge the cell state and hidden state.

Sample Program: Developing LSTM using Keras

Constructing an LSTM model in Keras is remarkably similar to building a Vanilla RNN. The primary difference lies in the layer you choose for the recurrent part of the network. In Keras, the LSTM layer is used to create LSTM networks. The basic steps for LSTM development include initializing the model, adding LSTM layers, and then compiling and fitting the model to your data.

Code Snippet for LSTM Model

Below is an example code snippet for constructing a simple LSTM network for sequence prediction:

```
from tensorflow.keras.models import Sequential
from tensorflow.keras.layers import LSTM, Dense

# Initialize the Sequential model
lstm_model = Sequential()
```

```
# Add an LSTM layer with 50 units, input shape (None, 10), and return_sequences=True
lstm_model.add(LSTM(50, input_shape=(None, 10), return_sequences=True))

# Add another LSTM layer with 50 units
lstm_model.add(LSTM(50))

# Add a Dense output layer with 1 unit (for regression)
lstm_model.add(Dense(1))

# Compile the model
lstm_model.compile(optimizer='adam', loss='mean_squared_error')

# Summary to display architecture
lstm_model.summary()
```

In this code example, we start by initializing a Sequential model, just like we did with the Vanilla RNN. The first layer added is an LSTM layer with 50 hidden units. Similar to the RNN example, the return_sequences=True parameter is crucial when stacking multiple LSTM layers, ensuring that the entire sequence is passed to the next layer. The final layer is a Dense layer with one unit, making this network suitable for regression tasks.

Model Compilation and Training

The compilation step is identical to what you've seen before; the model is compiled using the Adam optimizer and Mean Squared Error loss function. The training process, initiated by the fit method, also remains the same in structure, although training an LSTM might require more computational resources due to its complex architecture.

LSTMs bring a nuanced approach to handling sequence data, effectively tackling the challenges that plague Vanilla RNNs. Their ability to capture long-term dependencies makes them incredibly powerful for a wide array of applications, from natural language processing to financial forecasting. The advanced gating mechanisms enable LSTMs to learn what to remember and what to forget, providing them with a form of memory that is both long-term and short-term. These capabilities make LSTMs a go-to choice for many sequence modeling tasks, offering a robust and versatile solution for complex problems involving temporal data.

Introduction to Gated Recurrent Units (GRUs)

Gated Recurrent Units (GRUs), introduced by Cho et al. in 2014, represent another step in the evolution of recurrent neural networks. While LSTMs successfully addressed the shortcomings of Vanilla RNNs, their intricate design, involving multiple gates and states, often led to computational and resource-heavy models. GRUs aimed to simplify this architecture without significantly compromising the ability to capture long-term dependencies in sequence data. In many applications, GRUs have been found to perform almost as well as LSTMs but with fewer parameters, leading to quicker training times and reduced risk of overfitting.

Core Architectural Features of GRUs

A GRU network is similar to an LSTM network in that it also employs gating mechanisms to control the flow of information. However, it does so with less complexity. GRUs combine the cell state and the hidden state into a single state, and use only two gates: the update gate and the reset gate. The update gate determines how much of the previous state should be carried forward, similar to the combined role of the forget and input gates in an LSTM. The reset gate is used to control what portions of the previous state affect the new candidate state, akin to the role of the input gate in LSTMs.

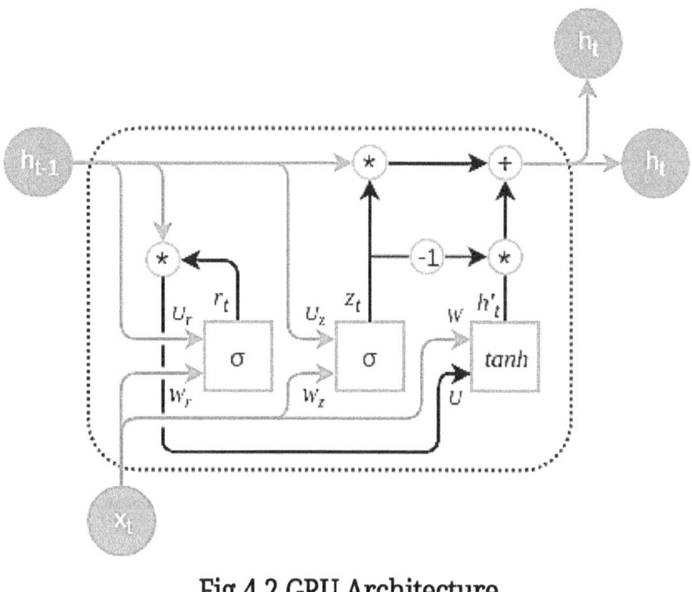

Fig 4.2 GRU Architecture

The update gate in a GRU performs a function akin to the forget and input gates in an LSTM but in a unified manner. It decides what to keep and what to discard from the previous hidden state. The reset gate allows the hidden state to optionally ignore the previous computed state and is particularly useful in forgetting irrelevant past information. These two gates, being fewer in number than in LSTMs, make GRUs computationally more efficient while still maintaining a similar level of effectiveness in learning from sequences.

Sample Program: Developing GRU Network

Constructing a GRU model in Keras follows a process similar to that of building LSTMs or Vanilla RNNs. You start by defining a sequential model and proceed to add layers. The key difference lies in the type of recurrent layer you choose to add, which, in this case, would be the GRU layer. Like with LSTMs, you then compile the model and fit it to your data.

Code Snippet for GRU Construction

Following is an example that demonstrates how to build a simple GRU network for sequence prediction using Keras:

```
from tensorflow.keras.models import Sequential
from tensorflow.keras.layers import GRU, Dense

# Initialize the Sequential model
gru_model = Sequential()

# Add a GRU layer with 50 units, input shape (None, 10)
gru_model.add(GRU(50, input_shape=(None, 10), return_sequences=True))

# Add another GRU layer with 50 units
gru_model.add(GRU(50))

# Add a Dense output layer with 1 unit (for regression)
gru_model.add(Dense(1))
```

```
# Compile the model
gru_model.compile(optimizer='adam', loss='mean_squared_error')

# Summary to display architecture
gru_model.summary()
```

The code starts with the familiar imports and the initialization of a Sequential model. The first layer added is a GRU layer with 50 units and an input shape that expects sequences of undefined length with 10 features. The return_sequences=True parameter ensures that the entire sequence is passed to the next layer, similar to what we saw with LSTMs and Vanilla RNNs. Finally, a Dense layer with one unit is added, making this model suitable for regression tasks.

The model is compiled using the Adam optimizer and Mean Squared Error loss function, just like the previous models. Training a GRU is also similar to training LSTMs and Vanilla RNNs, with the primary difference being that GRUs generally train faster due to their fewer parameters and simpler structure.

GRUs offer a middle ground between the simplicity of Vanilla RNNs and the complexity of LSTMs. They provide a more computationally efficient alternative to LSTMs while still capturing long-term dependencies effectively. This makes GRUs an attractive choice for tasks where resource utilization is a concern, but the complexity of the sequence data still requires advanced modeling. Understanding the mechanics and applications of GRUs enhances your toolkit for sequence modeling, giving you a broader range of options to tackle different types of problems in the domain of deep learning and sequence analysis.

RNNs in Time Series Analysis

Time series data involves observations on a variable or several variables over time. Examples include stock prices, weather data, and sales figures. What makes this type of data unique is its temporal dimension, which creates an inherent sequence within the data. RNNs, with their ability to capture temporal dependencies, are naturally suited for time series analysis. Unlike other machine learning algorithms that assume independence between observations, RNNs take into account the sequential nature of the data. The recurrent layers in an RNN can maintain state across different time steps, making them useful for capturing trends, seasonality, and other time-dependent structures within the data.

Role of RNNs in Forecasting and Anomaly Detection

In the realm of time series analysis, RNNs are commonly used for two broad categories of tasks: forecasting and anomaly detection.

- Forecasting involves predicting future values in a time series based on past observations. Given that RNNs can maintain state, they can be trained to make accurate forecasts even when the time series data have complex temporal dependencies like non-linear trends. Architectures like LSTMs help address vanishing gradient problems in plain RNNs.

- Anomaly detection, on the other hand, involves identifying unusual patterns that do not conform to expected behavior. Since RNNs can learn the sequence patterns in the training data, they can effectively detect anomalies and outliers in test data. Dual RNN architectures are sometimes used, with one RNN modeling normal behavior and the other detecting deviations.

Sample Program: RNN for Time Series Analysis

Dataset and Problem Statement

For this demonstration, let's assume we are using the open-source "Air Passengers" dataset, which contains monthly totals of international airline passengers from 1949 to 1960. Our objective is to forecast future passenger numbers based on past data. The dataset can be downloaded from the below URL:
https://github.com/kittenpub/database-repository/blob/main/AirPassengers.csv

Data Preprocessing

Before feeding the data into an RNN, the first step is to preprocess it. Typically, time series data may require normalization, and the sequence needs to be transformed into a supervised learning problem. Assuming we have our time series data in a Pandas DataFrame named df, we would normalize it as follows:

```
from sklearn.preprocessing import MinMaxScaler
```

```
scaler = MinMaxScaler(feature_range=(0, 1))
scaled_data = scaler.fit_transform(df)
```

After scaling, we would create sequences of a fixed length, say 3 months, to predict the passenger count for the next month. These sequences would serve as our input features, while the passenger count for the next month would be our label.

Building RNN Model

Building an RNN for time series analysis in Keras involves similar steps to what we've seen in previous demonstrations. Here is how you could define a simple RNN model for our problem:

```
from tensorflow.keras.models import Sequential
from tensorflow.keras.layers import SimpleRNN, Dense

# Initialize the model
time_series_model = Sequential()

# Add an RNN layer with 50 units and input shape (3, 1)
time_series_model.add(SimpleRNN(50, input_shape=(3, 1)))

# Add a Dense layer with 1 unit (for regression)
time_series_model.add(Dense(1))

# Compile the model
time_series_model.compile(optimizer='adam', loss='mean_squared_error')
```

Training and Evaluation

To train the model, you would use the sequences created during preprocessing as your input and fit the model using the fit method. Given that time series data is sequential, it's important to use the data in the correct temporal order during training. Evaluating the model would typically involve using metrics like RMSE (Root Mean Squared Error) on a validation set.

RNNs offer a powerful tool for modeling time series data due to their ability to capture sequential dependencies. This makes them particularly useful for complex tasks like forecasting and anomaly detection in time series analysis. However, one must carefully consider the choice of architecture, the length of sequences, and the preprocessing steps when designing an RNN for time series tasks. While Simple RNNs are a good starting point, more complex architectures like LSTMs and GRUs might be required for capturing longer-term dependencies in the data.

The Landscape of Text Generation Models

Introduction to Text Generation

Text generation is a subfield within Natural Language Processing (NLP) that focuses on generating human-like text based on a given input. The applications are numerous and include chatbots, machine translation, summarization, and creative writing tools, among others. Text generation models are typically a form of neural network specialized for handling language data. RNNs, LSTMs, and more recently, Transformer-based models like GPT (Generative Pre-trained Transformer) and BERT (Bidirectional Encoder Representations from Transformers), have been used for this purpose.

Architecture Choices for Text Generation

While RNNs and LSTMs have been historically significant for text generation, Transformer-based models are currently the state-of-the-art. They leverage self-attention mechanisms to consider the entire context, making them highly effective for language tasks. In contrast, RNNs and LSTMs look at sequences in a narrower, step-by-step manner, which can be a limitation for capturing long-term dependencies in language. Despite this, LSTMs and GRUs are still often used for simpler text generation tasks, thanks to their efficiency and lower computational demands.

Formation of Word Sequences

Role of Language Models

At the core of text generation lies a language model, which assigns probabilities to sequences of words. For example, given the input words "How are," a language model might assign a high probability to the next word being "you" and a low probability to it being "apple." These models are trained on vast corpora of text data to understand the statistical properties of a language. They essentially learn the likelihood of a word or sequence of words appearing in a given context within a language.

Mechanics of Sequence Formation

The simplest form of a language model could be an N-gram model, which uses the frequencies of sequences of 'N' words in the training data to predict the next word. However, N-gram models are generally poor at capturing the context when 'N' is small and become computationally expensive as 'N' increases. Neural network-based models like RNNs, LSTMs, and Transformers have effectively overcome these limitations. They can model complex patterns and long-term dependencies in text data, making them ideal for text generation tasks.

Decoding Strategies

Once the model is trained, the next step is to generate text, which involves selecting each subsequent word until a stop criterion is met. Various decoding strategies exist for this:

1. Greedy Decoding: The simplest approach, where the word with the highest probability is chosen at each step. While computationally efficient, it's not always the best for generating diverse or creative text.

2. Beam Search: A more sophisticated method where the model keeps track of multiple sequences (beams) at each step and extends the ones with the highest overall probabilities. This generally results in better quality but at a higher computational cost.

3. Random Sampling: In this method, the next word is sampled from the probability distribution of the predicted words. This introduces randomness and can generate more diverse sentences, but may sometimes produce irrelevant or incoherent text.

Attention Mechanisms and Contextual Embeddings

Modern text generation models often use attention mechanisms to weigh the importance of different parts of the input when making a prediction. This enables the model to focus on relevant parts of the text, improving the quality of the generated output. Furthermore, Transformer-based models like GPT and BERT generate contextual word embeddings, capturing semantic meanings and relationships between words, which significantly improves the quality of text generation.

Text generation is a blend of linguistic understanding and statistical modeling. The model needs to understand not just the syntax but also the semantics and context in which words are used. The advent of neural networks, especially architectures like LSTMs and Transformers, has revolutionized this field. They have enabled us to generate text that is not only syntactically correct but also contextually meaningful, opening up possibilities for more advanced and nuanced applications in natural language understanding and generation.

Attention Mechanism in RNNs

What is Attention?

In the context of neural networks, particularly RNNs, attention mechanisms help the model focus on certain parts of the input sequence when producing the output, much like how humans pay attention to specific portions of input when reading text or listening to someone. Originally developed to improve the performance of sequence-to-sequence models in tasks like machine translation, attention mechanisms have since been adapted for a variety of NLP tasks and have also been integrated into other types of neural networks.

Why Attention in RNNs?

RNNs are inherently good at handling sequences; however, their capability to remember long-range dependencies is limited. This limitation is particularly evident when sequences are long, leading to issues like the vanishing gradient problem. Attention mechanisms provide a solution by allowing the model to focus on different parts of the input sequence when generating each element of the output sequence. This makes the model more interpretable and enables it to capture long-range dependencies in the data, thus enhancing its performance.

Types of Attention Mechanisms

Several types of attention mechanisms exist, but the most commonly used ones are "Global Attention" and "Local Attention." In Global Attention, the model considers all the hidden states of the encoder RNN when computing the context vector. In contrast, Local Attention focuses on a subset of the hidden states. Advanced forms like "Multi-head Attention" and "Self-Attention" are also popular, especially in Transformer architectures, but for simplicity, we'll focus on a basic form of attention for integration into an RNN.

Sample Program: Adding Attention to RNN

Assuming we have a simple RNN model built using Keras for the time series analysis of the "Air Passengers" dataset from the below URL:
https://github.com/kittenpub/database-repository/blob/main/AirPassengers.csv

let's see how we can integrate an attention mechanism into it. We'll use Keras' built-in Attention layer for this purpose.

Code Snippet for RNN with Attention

Following is how you could modify a simple RNN model to include an attention mechanism:

```
from tensorflow.keras.models import Sequential
from tensorflow.keras.layers import SimpleRNN, Dense, Attention

# Initialize the model
model_with_attention = Sequential()

# Add an RNN layer with return sequences to true for attention
model_with_attention.add(SimpleRNN(50, return_sequences=True, input_shape=(3, 1)))

# Add Attention layer
model_with_attention.add(Attention())

# Add a Dense output layer
model_with_attention.add(Dense(1))

# Compile the model
model_with_attention.compile(optimizer='adam', loss='mean_squared_error')

# Display the model architecture
model_with_attention.summary()
```

Explanation of the Changes

In this modified model, after the initial SimpleRNN layer, we introduce an Attention layer. The SimpleRNN layer's return_sequences=True flag ensures that the full sequence of outputs is returned, which is necessary for the attention mechanism to compute the weighted sum of these outputs. The Attention layer then takes these sequences and computes the attention weights, effectively allowing the model to focus on different parts of the input sequence for each output element. Finally, a Dense layer is added for the actual prediction.

Benefits of Attention Mechanism

Integrating attention into RNNs provides several advantages. It improves the model's ability to focus on relevant parts of the input sequence, thereby capturing long-range dependencies more effectively. This is particularly beneficial in tasks where the input and output sequences can be of different lengths or where the alignment between the elements of the sequences is not known in advance, such as in machine translation or summarization.

Summary

In this chapter, we explored the capabilities of Recurrent Neural Networks (RNNs) and their applications in processing sequential data. We started by looking at the fundamental RNN architecture and how it maintains state across time steps through cyclical connections. This enables RNNs to model temporal context and long-term dependencies in data sequences. We learned more advanced RNN variants like LSTMs and GRUs which were designed to address the vanishing gradient problem faced by vanilla RNNs.

For text generation, we saw how RNN-based language models predict the next word by learning from extensive corpora. Transformer networks are now state-of-the-art, using self-attention to capture dependencies regardless of distance. We covered different decoding strategies like greedy search, beam search and sampling which affect the coherence of generated text.

Later, we looked at augmenting RNNs with attention mechanisms. Attention allows the model to focus on relevant parts of the input when making each output prediction. We implemented a simple attention-based RNN in Keras for time series forecasting. The hands-on examples provided practical experience in training and evaluating RNNs.

Overall, this chapter provided a comprehensive introduction to RNN architectures, highlighted their capabilities in processing sequential data, and demonstrated their real-world applications through concrete examples. The key takeaway is an understanding of how to effectively leverage RNNs and their extensions for problems involving sequential data across domains.

CHAPTER 5: DATA GENERATION WITH GENERATIVE ADVERSARIAL NETWORKS

Demand for Data Generation Technology

The escalating intricacies and expanding dimensions of contemporary machine learning models have precipitated an intense demand for voluminous, varied, and quality-rich datasets. This demand is propelled by the need to train models that are increasingly sophisticated, capable of navigating the nuanced and complex landscapes of today's data-driven challenges. Yet, the acquisition of such datasets is often a formidable endeavor, fraught with high costs, extensive time investments, and, in certain domains, a labyrinth of ethical considerations. Particularly in sensitive fields like healthcare, where the sanctity of patient confidentiality must be preserved, the direct collection of real-world data can traverse the bounds of practicality and ethicality. This conundrum has catalyzed the burgeoning interest in and necessity for advanced data generation technologies—innovations that can synthesize data which is not only realistic but also respects the privacy and ethical boundaries inherent in certain types of data.

Synthetic data generation emerges as a beacon of hope in this landscape, offering a dual advantage. It serves as an augmentative force, bolstering existing datasets with new, artificial data points, and as an explorative tool, simulating scenarios that have yet to manifest in the real world. Such capabilities are not just additive; they are transformative, providing critical insights that drive decision-making and enhance the predictive prowess of analytical models. However, the creation of synthetic data is far from a trivial pursuit. It demands a nuanced understanding of the data's essence, especially when dealing with complex structures or navigating the vastness of high-dimensional spaces. Conventional data augmentation techniques—such as image rotation, scaling, or flipping—fall short in their ability to conjure truly novel and diverse data points. While these methods can introduce variability, they often lack the depth and breadth required to fully train machine learning models.

Statistical methods, though adept at modeling certain aspects of a dataset's distribution, frequently stumble when confronted with the intricate patterns and interdependencies that characterize real-world data. These methods can replicate the shadow of the data but not its soul. In response, the frontier of data generation technology is being pushed by more sophisticated approaches. These advanced systems are engineered not just to mimic statistical properties but to delve deeper, capturing the subtle and intricate characteristics that define authentic data. They leverage cutting-edge techniques, including generative adversarial networks (GANs) and other forms of generative models, to produce data that is not only statistically consistent but also rich in the complexities and variabilities of real-world phenomena.

The promise of such technologies is vast, extending beyond mere data generation. They hold the potential to unlock new realms of possibility in machine learning, providing the fuel for models to learn, adapt, and evolve in ways previously unattainable. As the demand for synthetic data generation technology continues to surge, it stands as a testament to the ever-growing sophistication of machine learning and the unyielding quest for datasets that can keep pace with the relentless advancement of artificial intelligence.

Generative Adversarial Networks (GANs)

Introduction to GANs

Generative Adversarial Networks, or GANs, represent a class of artificial intelligence algorithms that have revolutionized the field of synthetic data generation since their inception by Ian Goodfellow and his team in 2014. At their core, GANs consist of two distinct neural networks that engage in a dynamic rivalry: the Generator, which is tasked with crafting data indistinguishable from a genuine dataset, and the Discriminator, which learns to discern between the authentic data and the forgeries created by the Generator.

The interplay between these two networks is akin to an intricate dance. The Generator begins by producing data that is initially likely to be rudimentary and easily detectable as fake. However, as the Discriminator becomes more adept at identifying the generated data, the Generator concurrently evolves, refining its output in an attempt to outwit its adversary. This adversarial process is iterative and competitive, propelling both networks towards improvement; the Generator strives to create data that is ever more lifelike, while the Discriminator hones its ability to detect subtleties that distinguish real data from imitations.

Capabilities of GANs

The versatility of GANs is nothing short of remarkable. In image generation, they have been instrumental in synthesizing photorealistic human portraits, artworks that echo the styles of renowned artists, and detailed medical imagery for academic inquiry. Beyond the visual sphere, GANs have ventured into the realm of text generation. Despite the inherent challenges posed by the discrete and complex structure of language, GANs have made strides in creating textual content, albeit with room for further refinement. Additionally, their utility extends to the generation of structured data, such as the tabular datasets vital to sectors like finance and healthcare, where they can simulate realistic scenarios for analysis and testing.

Transformative Impact

The impact of GANs on the field of machine learning and data science has been transformative. By generating synthetic data, GANs have enabled research and development in areas where data is scarce or sensitive. They have been integral in advancing fields like computer vision, natural language processing, and reinforcement learning, where large and complex datasets are often required for training robust models. The generated data can also be used for testing and validating models, thus ensuring that they are both accurate and robust before deployment.

Limitations and Ethical Considerations

However, the power of GANs comes with its own set of limitations and ethical considerations. Training a GAN requires significant computational resources, and the training process itself can be unstable, leading to problems like mode collapse. On the ethical front, the capability of GANs to generate realistic data raises concerns about their potential misuse, such as creating deepfakes that convincingly replace a person's likeness and voice in a video. Therefore, while GANs offer a compelling solution to the data generation problem, responsible usage and ongoing research to mitigate their limitations are imperative.

Architecture of GANs

Generative Adversarial Networks (GANs) represent a fascinating and potent class of neural networks with two distinct components: the Generator and the Discriminator. These components engage in a continuous game of cat-and-mouse, each improving in response to the other's performance, which is the hallmark of the adversarial training process that defines GANs.

The Generator

The Generator begins its process with a random noise vector, a seed of potential that contains within it the blueprint for new data. It's an artist with an evolving style, learning to mimic the complexities of real-world data distributions. Through a series of neural network layers, which can be as varied as the applications they serve, this component of the GAN refines its noise input into a synthetic masterpiece indistinguishable from actual data.

In the realm of imagery, the Generator might employ deconvolutional layers, which act as the artist's brushes, upsampling the noise to create intricate textures and patterns that form a coherent image. For the written word, it may use recurrent layers, weaving letters and words into sentences and stories, all from the seed of randomness it began with. The ultimate goal for the Generator is a state of deception so complete that the Discriminator loses its ability to discern the forged from the real.

The Discriminator

Opposite the Generator stands the Discriminator, a binary classifier whose sole purpose is to separate the wheat from the chaff, the real from the synthetic. This network serves as a critic, scrutinizing the outputs of the Generator alongside actual data. The architecture of the Discriminator is tailored to the task at hand; for images, it might be a convolutional neural network (CNN) that dissects the visual content layer by layer, searching for signs of forgery. For textual content, a recurrent neural network (RNN) might unravel sequences of text, looking for patterns that betray their artificial origins.

The Discriminator's mission is to hone its senses to such a fine point that it can reliably tell if the data it examines is a product of the Generator's imagination or a piece of reality. It's a detective, always on the lookout for the slightest clue that what it's seeing is not as it seems.

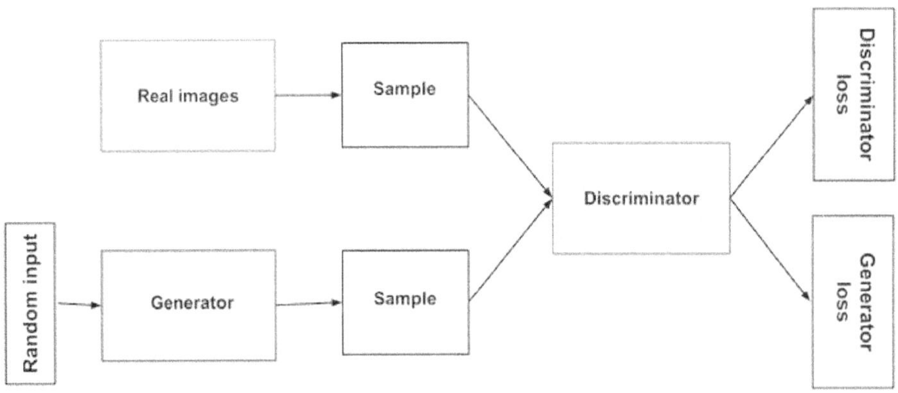

Fig 5.1 Generative Adversarial Network

The interplay between these two networks is a dance of complexity and subtlety. With each iteration of training, the Generator becomes more adept at creating data that can pass the Discriminator's increasingly stringent tests. In turn, the Discriminator grows more discerning, pushing the Generator to new heights of creativity. This adversarial tango is not just a competition but a collaboration that drives both networks towards perfection.

Essential Concepts in GANs

Adversarial Training

The adversarial process is the core of how GANs operate. It is a sophisticated form of training that pits two networks against each other in a game that resembles a forger trying to pass off their work as genuine, with an expert trying to catch the forgery. The Generator network takes on the role of the forger, learning to produce data that is increasingly difficult to distinguish from the real thing. Conversely, the Discriminator acts as the expert, refining its ability to detect the Generator's fakes. This process is dynamic, with both networks learning from each other's successes and failures, driving each other to improve iteratively.

Loss Functions

The performance of both the Generator and the Discriminator is quantified through loss functions, which play a critical role in the training process. These functions measure the success of each network in fulfilling its role. For the Discriminator, the loss function assesses its ability to correctly classify input as real or fake. For the Generator, the loss function evaluates how well it deceives the Discriminator into accepting the synthetic data as real. Binary cross-entropy loss is a popular choice for this purpose, providing a clear statistical measure of the divergence between the Discriminator's classifications and the ground truth.

Mode Collapse

Training GANs is not without its challenges. Mode collapse is a significant issue where the Generator discovers and exploits certain weaknesses in the Discriminator, leading to a lack of diversity in the generated data. This results in the Generator producing variations of the same output, which, while convincing to the Discriminator, fails to capture the rich variability of the real data distribution. To combat this, techniques such as minibatch discrimination, which encourages diversity among the generated samples, and gradient penalty, which enforces smoothness in the learning process, are employed.

Training Stability

Stability in training GANs is another critical issue. The adversarial training process can be delicate, with the potential for the training to diverge if the networks' learning rates and batch sizes are not carefully calibrated. This requires a meticulous approach to setting hyperparameters and may involve trial and error to find a stable configuration.

Conditional GANs and Advanced Variants

The versatility of GANs has led to the development of various advanced models that expand their capabilities. Conditional GANs (cGANs) introduce additional inputs that allow control over the generated data, enabling the creation of data that meets specific conditions or attributes. This has vast applications, such as in targeted data generation where specific features are desired, or in image-to-image translation tasks where an image of one type is transformed to match a particular style or characteristic.

Other variants like CycleGAN allow for the transformation of images from one domain to another without paired examples, opening up possibilities in areas such as style transfer and photo enhancement. Wasserstein GANs (WGANs) introduce a new loss function that improves training stability and provides a more reliable measure of the Generator's performance, addressing some of the challenges inherent in the original GAN framework.

Build Generators in Keras

We shall delve into the practical aspects of building a Generator using Keras. For this demonstration, we'll consider a simple task of generating handwritten digits, similar to the ones found in the MNIST dataset. We'll use the generator to transform random noise into recognizable digits. The MNIST dataset is commonly used for this kind of task and we have already used it in our previous chapters.

Importing Libraries

First, we'll import all the necessary libraries. For this example, we'll need Keras components for building the neural network, as well as NumPy for numerical operations. The code snippet below outlines these imports:

```
from tensorflow.keras.models import Sequential
from tensorflow.keras.layers import Dense, Reshape, BatchNormalization, UpSampling2D,
Conv2D
import numpy as np
```

Designing Generator Network

The architecture of the Generator will include dense layers followed by batch normalization layers and then upsampling layers to convert the random noise into a 2D image. Following is how you can build the Generator:

```
def build_generator(input_shape=(100,)):
    model = Sequential()
    model.add(Dense(128 * 7 * 7, activation='relu', input_shape=input_shape))
    model.add(Reshape((7, 7, 128)))
    model.add(BatchNormalization())
    model.add(UpSampling2D())
    model.add(Conv2D(128, kernel_size=3, padding='same', activation='relu'))
    model.add(BatchNormalization())
    model.add(UpSampling2D())
    model.add(Conv2D(1, kernel_size=3, padding='same', activation='tanh'))
    return model
```

The Generator starts with a dense layer that takes a 100-dimensional noise vector as input. This is then reshaped into a 7x7x128 tensor and passed through a batch normalization layer for stability. The UpSampling2D layers double the dimensions of the image, and these are followed by 2D convolution layers with ReLU activations. The final layer uses a tanh activation, ensuring the output values are within the range of -1 and 1, which is the typical practice for GANs.

Compiling Generator Model

Unlike Discriminators, Generators are not usually compiled independently as they are part of the broader GAN architecture. However, it's essential to understand the role of the loss function and optimizer in the overall GAN training loop. For Generators, the most commonly used loss function is binary cross-entropy, and the Adam optimizer is often the optimizer of choice.

Here, we have created a Generator network capable of taking a random noise vector of 100 dimensions and transforming it into a 2D image that mimics a handwritten digit. The use of upsampling and convolution layers enables the network to generate high-quality images from random noise. Batch normalization layers add stability, making the network easier to train.

To sum up, building a Generator in Keras involves choosing the appropriate architecture that can effectively transform random noise into meaningful data. The design choices for the layers, activations, and other components are often guided by the type of data you're looking to generate. The ultimate objective is to create a Generator that can produce data so convincing that it fools the Discriminator into thinking it's real. This sample demonstration serves as a perfect learning on constructing such a network using Keras.

Design Discriminators in Keras

Introduction to Discriminator Design

After going over the Generator, it is extremely important to get a grasp on its opposite, which is known as the Discriminator. The Discriminator acts as a judge, attempting to differentiate between data that is generated and data that is actually present in the world. In the context of our demonstration of the generation of handwritten digits, the Discriminator will determine, given an image of handwritten digits, whether or not it is an authentic sample from the MNIST dataset or an artificial creation of the Generator.

Libraries and Dependencies

Assuming that you imported Keras and any other necessary libraries while building the Generator, there is no need to import them again because doing so would be redundant. In the event that you do not, check that you have the following imports:

```
from tensorflow.keras.models import Sequential
from tensorflow.keras.layers import Dense, Flatten, Conv2D, LeakyReLU, Dropout
```

Constructing the Discriminator Network

When working with different types of data, the architecture of the Discriminator must frequently be adapted accordingly. A Convolutional Neural Network, also known as a CNN, is typically efficient when processing image data. The following steps will walk you through the construction of a basic Discriminator using Keras:

```
def build_discriminator(input_shape=(28, 28, 1)):
    model = Sequential()
    model.add(Conv2D(64, kernel_size=3, strides=2, padding='same',
input_shape=input_shape))
    model.add(LeakyReLU(alpha=0.2))
    model.add(Dropout(0.4))
    model.add(Conv2D(64, kernel_size=3, strides=2, padding='same'))
    model.add(LeakyReLU(alpha=0.2))
    model.add(Dropout(0.4))
    model.add(Flatten())
    model.add(Dense(1, activation='sigmoid'))
    return model
```

The Discriminator begins with a convolutional layer that has 64 filters and a kernel size of 3, and then it moves on to a Leaky ReLU activation function with a value of 0.2 for the alpha parameter. This particular alpha value enables the function to pass some gradient even when the unit being trained is inactive, which contributes to the network's improved capacity for learning. In order to prevent overfitting, the Dropout layer with a rate of 0.4 is added for the purpose of regularization. This architecture iterates one more time before flattening the output and sending it through a dense layer with a sigmoid activation. This layer will produce a probability value indicating whether or not the image is real.

Compiling the Discriminator

Since the Discriminator is a binary classifier, the binary cross-entropy was chosen to serve as the loss function when it was being compiled. Because of its high level of performance and relatively low memory requirements, the Adam optimizer is frequently utilized during the training process for GANs.

```
from tensorflow.keras.optimizers import Adam

discriminator = build_discriminator()
discriminator.compile(optimizer=Adam(0.0002, 0.5), loss='binary_crossentropy',
metrics=['accuracy'])
```

Critical Analysis

the Discriminator is an essential part of the overall architecture of the GAN. It puts the Generator's capabilities to the test, compelling it to get better at what it does and produce data that is harder and harder to tell apart from the real thing. Although it is an otherwise ordinary neural network, the Discriminator is an extremely important component of the adversarial training procedure. Both the design and the performance of the GAN model train can have a significant impact on how quickly and efficiently it operates. Therefore, anyone who is going to venture into the world of Generative Adversarial Networks needs to have a solid grasp of its construction as well as its function.

Training Strategies

The Adversarial Training Loop

Training a GAN is akin to a cat-and-mouse game between the Generator and the Discriminator. Unlike conventional neural networks where the model aims to minimize a loss function, GANs involve two loss functions: one for the Generator and another for the Discriminator. The training loop is an iterative process where each network's primary aim is to outperform the other. The Generator strives to generate data that the Discriminator cannot distinguish from real data, while the Discriminator aims to improve its ability to differentiate between real and generated samples. This adversarial nature leads to a dynamic equilibrium, ideally resulting in a Generator capable of creating data almost indistinguishable from real data.

Data Batching and Labeling

One key aspect of GAN training is the manner in which data is presented to the model. Typically, training data is divided into batches. Each batch contains a mix of real data and synthetic data generated by the Generator. Real data is usually labeled with ones, and generated data with zeros, adhering to the binary classification task of the Discriminator. This becomes an important strategy as the Discriminator needs to learn from both real and fake data samples. Effective data batching can significantly impact the Discriminator's training efficiency, and subsequently the Generator's ability to produce realistic data.

Loss Function Tuning

In the standard GAN setup, binary cross-entropy is commonly used for both the Generator and the Discriminator. However, there are variations of loss functions tailored for specific types of GANs or to solve particular problems. For instance, the Wasserstein loss is often used in Wasserstein GANs to provide more stable and meaningful loss metrics. Similarly, Least Squares GANs use least squares loss functions to push generated data to resemble a Gaussian distribution. The choice of loss function is not arbitrary and needs to be aligned with the goals of the GAN model. Experimenting with different loss functions can sometimes yield dramatically different results, making this an essential strategy in GAN training.

Hyperparameter Optimization

The training of GANs is highly sensitive to the choice of hyperparameters. These include the learning rates for the Generator and the Discriminator, batch sizes, and the architecture of the neural networks. While Adam is the optimizer of choice for many GANs, tweaking its parameters like learning rate and beta values can have a considerable impact. For instance, different learning rates for the Generator and the Discriminator can sometimes help avoid issues like mode collapse, where the Generator generates only a subset of plausible data. Grid search or random search methods are often employed to find the optimal set of hyperparameters.

Dealing with Mode Collapse and Instability

GAN training presents a number of significant challenges, two of which are mode collapse and training instability. The mode collapses when the Generator discovers a way to trick the Discriminator by only generating a small amount of data. This causes the Discriminator to become confused. In order to circumvent this issue, a number of solutions, such as minibatch discrimination and adding noise to the labels produced by the Discriminator (label smoothing), have been developed. Instability in training often takes the form of oscillations in the loss function, which makes it difficult to determine whether or not the system has converged. The training process can be made more stable with the help of techniques such as gradient clipping and architectural adjustments such as adding skip connections.

Monitoring and Evaluation Metrics

It is absolutely necessary to have metrics at one's disposal while training a GAN in order to evaluate the effectiveness of both the Generator and the Discriminator. In contrast to supervised learning models, which typically employ metrics such as accuracy or F1-score, GANs call for the use of more nuanced metrics. It is common practice to employ Frechet Inception Distance (FID) and Inception Score when attempting to quantify the quality of samples that have been generated. Monitoring these metrics while the model is being trained can provide valuable insights into the performance of the model and is often essential for hyperparameter tuning and model selection.

In conclusion, training a GAN is a complicated process that calls for an in-depth knowledge of a variety of strategies. These strategies range from the architecture and loss functions to the hyperparameter tuning and evaluation metrics. Because GANs are inherently adversarial, their training presents a problem that is both challenging and fascinating.

Introduction to Conditional GANs

Conditional Generative Adversarial Networks, or cGANs, represent an evolution of the Generative Adversarial Network paradigm, introducing a conditional aspect to the generation process. This advancement allows for the generation of data that is not just convincing but also tailored to specific conditions or parameters, such as class labels, tags, or even other data points.

Concept of Conditionality in GANs

In a standard GAN, the Generator creates data from a latent space of random noise, learning the distribution of the training data. However, this process lacks direction; the Generator has no control over the type of data it produces. cGANs address this by incorporating additional conditional information, effectively guiding the data generation process.

For example, in a dataset of animal images, a regular GAN might generate random animal pictures without any specific order or preference. In contrast, a cGAN can be conditioned to generate images of a 'cat' when provided with the corresponding label. This is achieved by feeding the condition into both the Generator and the Discriminator.

Enhancing Generator and Discriminator with Conditions

In a cGAN, the Generator receives both a random noise vector and a conditional input. This could be a one-hot encoded vector representing class labels in classification tasks or any other form of relevant information. The Generator then learns to craft data that is not only realistic but also satisfies the given condition.

The Discriminator, too, is conditioned with the same label or data. It receives pairs of data and conditions and must determine the authenticity of the data under the given condition. This dual conditioning fundamentally changes the learning dynamics, as the Discriminator can no longer base its decisions solely on the data's realism; it must also consider the relevance of the data to the condition.

Sample Program: Implementing cGAN

Required Libraries and Dataset

You do not need to import TensorFlow or any of the other necessary modules again if you did so when you were building the basic GAN. This is because you have already imported them. We shall pretend for the sake of this demonstration that we want to generate MNIST handwritten digits conditionally based on their labels.

Constructing the Conditional Generator

In a cGAN, the Generator requires both a noise vector and a label in order to function properly. Before inserting them into the network, we join these two together to form a single string. An abbreviated version of the code is as follows:

```
from tensorflow.keras.layers import Concatenate

def build_conditional_generator(z_dim, label_dim):
    model = Sequential()
    model.add(Dense(128, input_dim=(z_dim + label_dim)))
    model.add(LeakyReLU(0.01))
    model.add(Dense(784, activation='tanh'))
    return model

# Usage
z_dim = 100
label_dim = 10
```

```
generator = build_conditional_generator(z_dim, label_dim)

noise = tf.random.normal((1, z_dim))
label = tf.one_hot([7], depth=label_dim)  # One-hot encoding for digit '7'
input_data = Concatenate(axis=1)([noise, label])
generated_data = generator(input_data)
```

Constructing the Conditional Discriminator

In a manner analogous to that of the Generator, the Discriminator accepts the data as well as the label as input. We are able to adapt the current Discriminator so that it can take in this concatenated input.

```
def build_conditional_discriminator(img_shape, label_dim):
    model = Sequential()
    model.add(Dense(128, input_dim=(np.prod(img_shape) + label_dim)))
    model.add(LeakyReLU(0.01))
    model.add(Dense(1, activation='sigmoid'))
    return model

# Usage
img_shape = (28, 28, 1)
discriminator = build_conditional_discriminator(img_shape, label_dim)

real_data = tf.random.normal((1, np.prod(img_shape)))
input_data = Concatenate(axis=1)([real_data, label])
validity = discriminator(input_data)
```

Training the Conditional GAN

Training a cGAN is similar to training a regular GAN, but with the additional step of feeding the labels into both the Generator and the Discriminator. During each iteration, the Generator creates data based on a random noise vector and a label, and the Discriminator evaluates the authenticity of real and generated data based on the corresponding labels.

To sum up, Conditional GANs provide a process for the generation of data that is more tightly controlled by the introduction of conditional variables that direct the Generator and the Discriminator. In order to accommodate these conditional variables during the practical implementation of a cGAN in TensorFlow, the Generator and Discriminator will need to undergo some minor but essential modifications. Because of this, the capabilities of the GAN architecture have been significantly expanded, and the result is a model that is more flexible and able to generate particular kinds of data.

Advanced Data Augmentation for GANs

Role of Data Augmentation in GANs

In the fields of machine learning and deep learning, data augmentation is a technique that is essential, and the significance of this technique is not diminished when learning Generative Adversarial Networks (GANs). The robustness of both the Generator and the Discriminator can be improved with the help of data augmentation techniques, which can be particularly useful in this regard. Data augmentation is a process that can lead to more stable GAN training and the generation of higher-quality synthetic data. This process involves artificially increasing the size and diversity of the training dataset through a variety of transformations. The application of data augmentation in GANs, on the other hand, goes beyond the basic methods such as rotation and scaling that are frequently used in conventional neural networks.

Spatial Augmentations

In the context of GANs, particularly those responsible for the generation of images, spatial transformations can be of tremendous assistance. Training general artificial neural networks (GANs) to generate handwritten characters can make use of more advanced techniques such as elastic transformations, which mimic the natural variation that occurs in handwriting. The image is first resized to be larger than the target size, and then it is randomly cropped from that larger version. Random jittering is yet another method. These methods can give the network spatial invariance, which strengthens its resistance to varying data types and formats and makes the network more flexible.

Color Space Manipulations

Alterations to the color space are yet another method for achieving advanced data augmentation. Data can be augmented in a nuanced manner through the use of methods such as histogram equalization, which boosts the contrast of an image, or channel-wise normalization, which provides more accurate readings. These techniques have the potential to provide a more difficult training environment for GANs that are used in tasks such as style transfer or colorization. This environment will encourage the Generator to learn more effective transformations. Jittering the colors of an image, which involves making random adjustments to the brightness, contrast, and saturation of the image, can also be useful. When the dataset has variable lighting conditions or when the generated content needs to adapt to different color profiles, these manipulations can be especially important.

Temporal Augmentations for Sequence Data

Temporal augmentations can be extremely helpful when working with GANs that were developed specifically for sequence generation (for example, video or time-series data). The general artificial network (GAN) can be made more resilient to fluctuations in speed and the absence of data through the use of techniques such as time warping and time masking. Time warping involves stretching or compressing the timeline of a sequence, while time masking involves setting a portion of the sequence to zero. These are more advanced methods that are typically utilized in fields such as speech recognition and natural language processing, but they are amenable to modification for use in GANs that are concerned with the generation of data of a similar nature.

Augmentation in Latent Space

The capability of GANs to perform data augmentation in the latent space is one of the features that sets them apart from other machine learning methods. Altering the random noise that is fed into the Generator can be done in place of changing the data itself. For instance, making minute adjustments to the noise vector can result in the production of a wide variety of distinct samples that are all closely related to one another. This can assist in diversifying the samples that are generated without having an effect on the distribution of the actual data, thereby making the GAN more resistant to overfitting. In addition to this, it makes it possible to investigate data distributions that are more intricate and multifaceted, which forces the Generator and the Discriminator to develop further.

Adversarial Augmentation

One more intriguing strategy is to employ adversarial training for the data augmentation process in and of itself. It is possible to include adversarial examples in the training data. These are examples that are purposefully created in order to trick the model. Because of this, the Discriminator is challenged to enhance its classification capabilities, which in turn forces the Generator to produce data that is more representative of the real world. In practice, this results in the formation of an improvement feedback loop in which the Generator and the Discriminator continually improve their skills, which ultimately results in a GAN model that is more robust and efficient.

Data augmentation in the realm of GANs is a multi-faceted and rich field that offers numerous avenues for improving model performance. From spatial and color transformations to temporal and latent space manipulations, each technique offers unique advantages and challenges. These advanced methods can significantly impact the quality of the generated data and the stability of the training process.

Neural Style Transfer

What is Neural Style Transfer?

In the fields of computer vision and machine learning, a technique known as Neural Style Transfer (NST) combines two images—a content image and a style image—to produce a new, synthesized output that maintains the content of the original image while adopting the artistic style of the other. This technique creates a new, synthesized output that retains the content of the original image while adopting the artistic style of the other. The method utilizes the power of Convolutional Neural Networks (CNNs), in particular pre-trained networks such as VGG-19, to split and recombine the subject matter and aesthetic of individual images. The ability of NST to push the boundaries of what is possible with machine learning has gotten the company a lot of attention. NST offers a blend of art and technology that is mesmerizing and technically impressive at the same time.

The Fundamental Mechanistic Principles

The fundamental idea behind NST is based on the capability of isolating specific content and style features within an image. This is made possible by the numerous layers that CNNs contain. The deeper layers of the network are typically responsible for capturing the content features; these are the layers in which high-level features such as object shapes are represented. On the other hand, the shallow layers are where style characteristics are stored, and they represent different patterns and textures. During NST, a loss function will be defined, and it will consist of three parts: the loss of content, the loss of style, and the loss of total variation. The content loss ensures that the generated image is similar to the original content, the style loss ensures that the generated image adopts the style of the reference image, and the total variation loss provides the final output with a level of smoothness.

Common Use-cases

- The most straightforward implementation of NST can currently be found in the field of digital art. NST has been used to create stunning works that blend a variety of styles, ranging from traditional to modern. These pieces have been created by graphic designers and artists. In addition to being used in individual works of art, NST has also been implemented in the fields of film and animation. For instance, the technology has been utilized to recreate paintings by well-known artists in the style of movie scenes, as well as to produce one-of-a-kind visual effects that would be extremely time-consuming and laborious to produce manually.

- Surprisingly, NST has applications in fields other than the arts domain. The NST has been put to use in the realm of scientific research to improve the visibility of various medical images. For instance, medical practitioners and radiologists can improve their ability to diagnose conditions by copying the style of an existing medical image that has been thoroughly annotated and applying it to a new image that is less clear. To continue along this line of thought, NST can be utilized in microscopy to bring attention to particular aspects of microscopic images, which can be of assistance to researchers working in fields such as biology and materials science.

- NST provides a novel approach to the personalization of products for the retail industry. For instance, users can apply their preferred art style to articles of clothing or accessories by using an app, and businesses can produce these personalized items on demand. Users can also apply their preferred art style to other items. Because of NST, we are now able to achieve a level of personalization that was previously unimaginable but is now entirely possible. Similarly, NST can be used in interior design to generate wallpapers or textiles that match the aesthetic preferences of the customer, offering a highly personalized design experience. This can be done by matching the customer's aesthetic preferences to the customer's NST data.

The incredible potential of today's machine learning algorithms is brought to light by the groundbreaking project known as Neural Style Transfer. By bringing together the worlds of art and technology, NST paves the way for new possibilities in both the realms of creative expression and practical application. The technology has a broad range of use-cases that continue to expand as the underlying algorithms become more advanced. Some of these use-cases include the generation of mesmerizing art pieces, the enhancement of medical imaging, and the offering of unprecedented customization in retail. Other use-cases include offering unprecedented customization in retail. NST, however, comes with its own set of challenges and ethical considerations that society will need to address as the technology matures. These challenges and considerations are similar to those that come with any other powerful tool.

Implement NST Using TensorFlow

Setting up Environment and Dataset

TensorFlow will serve as our deep learning framework and will be utilized in the implementation of Neural Style Transfer. According to what was covered earlier, TensorFlow and Keras should already be installed in the environment in which you run Python. Images taken from the COCO dataset will serve as the demonstration's content, while well-known works of art will serve as the demonstration's style. Access to the COCO dataset, which is utilized extensively in the field of computer vision research, can be made available from the below URL:
https://cocodataset.org/#home

Preprocessing the Images

The pre-processing of the content and style images is the first step in the implementation of the solution. Both of the images need to have their dimensions adjusted so that they are the same, and their pixel values need to be standardized. TensorFlow offers a comprehensive set of functions that can handle the loading and preprocessing of images.

```
from tensorflow.keras.preprocessing import image as kp_image

def load_and_process_image(image_path):
    img = kp_image.load_img(image_path, target_size=(512, 512))
    img = kp_image.img_to_array(img)
    img = np.expand_dims(img, axis=0)
    img = tf.keras.applications.vgg19.preprocess_input(img)
    return img
```

Building the Model

We'll use the VGG19 model, pre-trained on the ImageNet dataset, as our base model. Specifically, we'll use the intermediate layers of the model to capture the content and style representations of the input images. We won't need the fully connected layers at the top of the model.

```
from tensorflow.keras.applications import VGG19

def get_model():
    model = VGG19(include_top=False, weights='imagenet')
    model.trainable = False
    return model
```

Defining Content and Style Layers

For the content layers, we generally use blocks from the deeper parts of the network, while for the style layers, we use blocks from the initial layers. This is because deeper layers capture high-level features (content), while the initial layers capture textures and colors (style).

```
content_layers = ['block5_conv2']
style_layers = ['block1_conv1', 'block2_conv1', 'block3_conv1', 'block4_conv1', 'block5_conv1']
```

Loss Functions and Optimization

In order to train the model, we define three different kinds of loss: total variation loss, style loss, and content loss. Because of the content loss, the generated image is guaranteed to keep the same content characteristics as the original image. The style loss ensures that the style characteristics of the style image are carried over into the image that is generated. Last but not least, the total variation loss contributes a degree of smoothness to the image that was generated. In order to minimize the amount of data that is lost, we will use TensorFlow's GradientTape to compute the gradients, and then we will use those gradients to update our content image.

```
optimizer = tf.optimizers.Adam(learning_rate=0.02, beta_1=0.99, epsilon=1e-1)
```

Executing Style Transfer

The entire style transfer is carried out inside of a loop, and in order to reduce the amount of loss function that occurs, we perform forward and backward passes. Following a predetermined number of iterations, we will have our final generated image, which will combine the subject matter and aesthetic of the two images that were input.

```
@tf.function()
def train_step(image, model, optimizer):
    with tf.GradientTape() as tape:
        # Forward pass
        # Compute losses
    # Backward pass
    gradients = tape.gradient(loss, image)
    optimizer.apply_gradients([(gradients, image)])
    image.assign(tf.clip_by_value(image, 0.0, 255.0))
```

Putting into practice Neural Style Transfer requires a number of steps, including the configuration of the environment and the pre-processing of images, as well as the definition of the neural network and the loss functions that are used for optimization. The final step is the execution of the style transfer, which involves the use of optimization techniques to produce an image that successfully combines the content and style of two separate images. You will be able to explore the fascinating world of Neural Style Transfer with the help of easily accessible datasets and resources thanks to this practical implementation, which was built on top of TensorFlow.

Summary

In this chapter, we dove headfirst into the fascinating world of Generative Adversarial Networks (GANs) and Neural Style Transfer, investigating both the theoretical underpinnings and the application of these technologies in the real world. GANs were presented as powerful tools that are able to generate synthetic data, and their architecture and training strategies were elaborated upon throughout the presentation. We were shown how to conceptualize and put into practice advanced data augmentation strategies for GANs, as well as how to construct generators and discriminators using the Keras programming language. The chapter came to a close with a practical walkthrough to the creation of a GAN, which emphasized the significance of various components such as loss functions and training strategies.

Neural Style Transfer (NST), which has the ability to blend the content and style of images, was another focus of this chapter. It captivated our imagination with its ability to do so. We discovered that NST separates and recombines the content and style characteristics of images by utilizing Convolutional Neural Networks, in particular pre-trained models such as VGG-19. The versatility of NST is demonstrated by the fact that its applications can be found not only in the field of digital art but also in scientific research, healthcare, and retail. Insights into the implementation of NST using TensorFlow were provided in the form of a detailed walkthrough. This chapter covered everything from establishing the environment and preprocessing images to defining the neural network and loss functions for optimization.

Additionally, the chapter placed an emphasis on the practical applications of these technologies as well as the ethical considerations associated with them. GANs, for instance, have applications in a variety of fields, such as the healthcare industry, where they can be used to enhance medical imaging, and the retail industry, where they offer one-of-a-kind ways to customize products. NST comes with its own unique set of challenges, some of which include high computational costs and difficult moral conundrums concerning artistic ownership.

CHAPTER 6: TRANSFORMERS FOR COMPLEX TASKS

Understanding Transformer Architecture

Basic Building Blocks

In recent years, natural language processing (NLP) and other sequence-related tasks have seen an explosion in interest in a particular class of models known as transformers. The self-attention mechanism and the position encoding are at the heart of the architecture of the transformer. These two components process sequences in conjunction with one another. Transformers, in contrast to Recurrent Neural Networks (RNNs) and Convolutional Neural Networks (CNNs), do not inherently understand the temporal or spatial dimensions of the sequence. In order to provide the model with some information regarding the position of each element within the sequence, positional encodings are appended to the input embeddings.

Self-Attention Mechanism

The self-attention mechanism is one of the most distinguishing characteristics of transformers. This mechanism enables the model to take into consideration other elements in the input sequence when it is processing a particular element. This is fundamentally different from RNNs, in which the hidden state stores information about previous elements in the sequence but not information about future elements, and from CNNs, which use filters to capture local features but frequently struggle with long-range dependencies. Transformers are ideally suited for tasks like language modeling, machine translation, and text summarization as a result of their ability to perform self-attention and, more specifically, multi-head self-attention. This enables transformers to efficiently manage long-range dependencies in the data.

Encoder-Decoder Structure

Encoders and decoders are the two components that make up the transformer model. Encoders are responsible for processing the data that is input, and decoders are responsible for producing the output. Each of these is composed of multiple layers—commonly six or more—of feed-forward and self-attention neural networks. When compared to the architecture of RNNs and CNNs, this is a striking departure. RNNs have a recurrent structure, which means that each element in the sequence is processed one at a time. Because of this, it can be challenging to run RNNs in parallel. CNNs, on the other hand, are built to process grid-like data such as images and do not have a natural way to handle sequence data without requiring modifications. This is because CNNs were initially designed to process image data. Due to the encoder-decoder structure of transformers as well as their self-attention mechanism, they are highly parallelizable, which in turn leads to shorter training times.

Positional Encoding

As mentioned earlier, transformers do not have a built-in sense of sequence or order. While RNNs inherently understand sequence due to their recurrent nature, and CNNs understand spatial hierarchies through their convolutional layers, transformers need an additional component to understand the order of elements in a sequence. This is achieved through positional encodings, which are added to the input embeddings before they are fed into the model. The positional encodings can be either learned by the model or fixed, but they are crucial for the model to make sense of sequences, especially for tasks like machine translation where the order of words is important.

Scalability and Flexibility

One of the key advantages of transformers over both RNNs and CNNs is their scalability. The self-attention mechanism allows transformers to efficiently handle long sequences, and their highly parallelizable architecture makes them adaptable to a variety of hardware configurations. This has led to the development of extremely large transformer models like GPT-3 and BERT, which consist of hundreds of millions or even billions of parameters. These large models have set new benchmarks in a wide range of NLP tasks, from text classification and language understanding to translation and summarization.

In a nutshell, the processing of sequence data has undergone a fundamental shift as a result of the introduction of transformers. Their one-of-a-kind architecture, which includes self-attention mechanisms and positional encodings, differentiates them from RNNs and CNNs in terms of their capabilities as well as the constraints they are subject to. Transformers offer a method of sequence modeling that is more adaptable and scalable in comparison to RNNs and CNNs. RNNs are great for tasks that require an understanding of the temporal dynamics of the data, and CNNs are excellent at capturing local and hierarchical features in grid-like data.

Working of Self-Attention Mechanism

Mathematics behind Self-Attention

The self-attention mechanism is at the heart of transformer architectures, and the way sequence data is processed is fundamentally altered as a result of its implementation. The Query (Q), the Key (K), and the Value (V) are the three components that make up each element in the sequence, according to the fundamental mathematical premise that underpins the concept of self-attention. These are obtained by multiplying the input embeddings by weight matrices that are discovered through training. This process is known as learning. After that, the attention score is determined by taking the dot product of the query and the key, which is then reduced in size, passed through a Softmax function, and used to determine the weights. The output, in its final form, is a weighted sum of the values.

Code for Self-Attention in TensorFlow

We shall take a look at the different ways self-attention can be implemented in TensorFlow:

```
import tensorflow as tf
import numpy as np

def scaled_dot_product_attention(q, k, v, mask=None):
    matmul_qk = tf.matmul(q, k, transpose_b=True)
    d_k = tf.cast(tf.shape(k)[-1], tf.float32)
    scaled_attention_logits = matmul_qk / tf.math.sqrt(d_k)
    if mask is not None:
        scaled_attention_logits += (mask * -1e9)
    attention_weights = tf.nn.softmax(scaled_attention_logits, axis=-1)
    output = tf.matmul(attention_weights, v)
    return output, attention_weights
```

In this code snippet, q, k, and v represent Query, Key, and Value, respectively. The attention scores are scaled by the square root of the dimension of the Key vectors (d_k). This is followed by the application of the Softmax function to obtain the attention weights, which are then used to get the weighted sum of the Value vectors, producing the output.

The self-attention mechanism shines in tasks that involve understanding the context between different parts of an input sequence. For instance, in machine translation, capturing the relationship between words that are far apart in a sentence is critical. While RNNs struggle with long-range dependencies due to vanishing and exploding gradient problems, and CNNs are limited by the receptive field of their filters, the self-attention mechanism can easily relate distant words to each other, making transformers particularly effective for such tasks.

Multi-Head Self-Attention

Even though the fundamental mechanism of self-attention is quite effective, the idea of multi-head self-attention takes things to an even higher level. In this variation, the model learns multiple sets of Query, Key, and Value weight matrices, and it attends to different parts of the input simultaneously. In order to generate the final result, the outputs generated by each 'head' are concatenated together and then linearly transformed. Because of this, the model is able to concentrate on various facets of the input, which increases the power of its representation.

```
class MultiHeadAttention(tf.keras.layers.Layer):
  def __init__(self, d_model, num_heads):
    super(MultiHeadAttention, self).__init__()
    self.num_heads = num_heads
    self.d_model = d_model
    assert d_model % self.num_heads == 0
    self.depth = d_model // self.num_heads
    self.wq = tf.keras.layers.Dense(d_model)
    self.wk = tf.keras.layers.Dense(d_model)
    self.wv = tf.keras.layers.Dense(d_model)
    self.dense = tf.keras.layers.Dense(d_model)
```

In this code snippet for multi-head self-attention, separate dense layers are used to transform the input into multiple Query, Key, and Value representations, and these are then passed through the self-attention mechanism defined earlier.

Transforming NLP Tasks with Self-Attention

The self-attention mechanism has been essential to the success of transformer models in a wide variety of NLP tasks, and this contribution has been widely recognized. For the task of abstractive text summarization, for instance, the mechanism enables the model to concentrate on the most important aspects of a lengthy document. This is something that was difficult for RNNs and CNNs to do. Similarly, self-attention enables the model to relate different parts of a context document with the query in question-answering systems, which frequently results in more accurate answers.

The self-attention mechanism's capacity to capture long-range dependencies in sequence data has ushered in a new era of innovation in the field of natural language processing (NLP). It overcomes the restrictions imposed by RNNs and CNNs, making it possible to process sequences in a manner that is both more flexible and effective. This mechanism has enabled transformers to set new benchmarks in a variety of complex tasks, firmly establishing them as the go-to model architecture for modern applications of NLP. Whether in its basic form or as multi-head self-attention, this mechanism has empowered transformers to set new benchmarks.

Sample Program: Implement TF-Transformers

We'll proceed to implement a transformer using TensorFlow and the previously referred MNIST dataset. The MNIST dataset consists of 28x28 grayscale images, but for the sake of demonstration, we'll consider each row of pixels as a sequence element, making each image a sequence of 28 elements. This way, we can utilize the transformer architecture for sequence modeling in a non-traditional domain, showcasing its versatility.

Initialization and Positional Encoding

We shall begin by generating the positional encoding, shall we? When constructing transformers, positional encodings are appended to the input embeddings. This action supplies the model with information regarding the sequence's position. This is extremely important because, unlike RNNs, transformers do not have a sequence processing mechanism already built into their architecture.

```
def get_angles(pos, i, d_model):
    angle_rates = 1 / np.power(10000, (2 * (i//2)) / np.float32(d_model))
    return pos * angle_rates

def positional_encoding(position, d_model):
    angle_rads = get_angles(np.arange(position)[:, np.newaxis],
                            np.arange(d_model)[np.newaxis, :],
                            d_model)
    angle_rads[:, 0::2] = np.sin(angle_rads[:, 0::2])
```

```
    angle_rads[:, 1::2] = np.cos(angle_rads[:, 1::2])
    pos_encoding = angle_rads[np.newaxis, ...]
    return tf.cast(pos_encoding, dtype=tf.float32)
```

Building the Encoder

The encoder of the transformer is made of a stack of identical layers, each consisting of a multi-head self-attention mechanism followed by a position-wise fully connected feed-forward network. Below is a simplified code snippet for constructing the encoder.

```
from tensorflow.keras.layers import LayerNormalization, Dense

class EncoderLayer(tf.keras.layers.Layer):
  def __init__(self, d_model, num_heads, dff, rate=0.1):
    super(EncoderLayer, self).__init__()

    self.mha = MultiHeadAttention(d_model, num_heads)
    self.ffn = tf.keras.Sequential([
      Dense(dff, activation='relu'),
      Dense(d_model)
    ])

    self.layernorm1 = LayerNormalization(epsilon=1e-6)
    self.layernorm2 = LayerNormalization(epsilon=1e-6)
```

Building the Decoder

When compared to the encoder, the decoder possesses an additional layer that is specifically designed to attend to the encoder's output. Following is the version with fewer details:

```
class DecoderLayer(tf.keras.layers.Layer):
  def __init__(self, d_model, num_heads, dff, rate=0.1):
    super(DecoderLayer, self).__init__()
```

```
self.mha1 = MultiHeadAttention(d_model, num_heads)
self.mha2 = MultiHeadAttention(d_model, num_heads)

self.ffn = tf.keras.Sequential([
  Dense(dff, activation='relu'),
  Dense(d_model)
])

self.layernorm1 = LayerNormalization(epsilon=1e-6)
self.layernorm2 = LayerNormalization(epsilon=1e-6)
self.layernorm3 = LayerNormalization(epsilon=1e-6)
```

Assembling the Transformer

The very last thing that needs to be done is to stack a number of encoder and decoder layers in order to complete the assembly of the transformer. In addition to this, we will also incorporate the final linear layer of the MNIST dataset, which is the layer that generates logits for each class.

```
class Transformer(tf.keras.Model):
  def __init__(self, num_layers, d_model, num_heads, dff, input_vocab_size,
         target_vocab_size, rate=0.1):
    super(Transformer, self).__init__()

    self.encoder = Encoder(num_layers, d_model, num_heads, dff,
               input_vocab_size, rate)
    self.decoder = Decoder(num_layers, d_model, num_heads, dff,
               target_vocab_size, rate)
    self.final_layer = Dense(target_vocab_size)
```

Following the completion of the assembly of the transformer, the subsequent steps consist of compiling the model, establishing the training loop, and, as a final step, testing the model using the MNIST dataset.

When compared to conventional sequence models, you will notice that the transformer trains significantly more quickly and, in many cases, achieves superior performance. This is made possible by its parallel architecture.

The demonstration that was just shown illustrates how versatile and powerful transformers can be. Their architecture is well-suited for a variety of sequence modeling tasks, including image classification, despite the fact that they were initially designed for text-based tasks. As we've seen, this includes text-based tasks. Transformers are one of the most powerful tools in the machine learning toolkit thanks to their adaptability.

Training and Testing the Transformer

Model Compilation

Once the Transformer model is built, it needs to be compiled with a loss function, optimizer, and evaluation metric before the training process starts. Given that MNIST is a classification problem with 10 classes, we'll use Sparse Categorical Cross-Entropy as the loss function. The Adam optimizer is generally a good choice for transformers.

```
from tensorflow.keras.optimizers import Adam
from tensorflow.keras.losses import SparseCategoricalCrossentropy

loss_object = SparseCategoricalCrossentropy(from_logits=True, reduction='none')
optimizer = Adam(learning_rate=0.001)

transformer.compile(optimizer=optimizer, loss=loss_object, metrics=['accuracy'])
```

Through TensorFlow, the MNIST dataset can also be accessed with relative ease rather than loading from URL. After loading the data, we will first normalize it and then reformat it so that it is compatible with the transformer model.

```
mnist = tf.keras.datasets.mnist
(train_images, train_labels), (test_images, test_labels) = mnist.load_data()
train_images = train_images / 255.0
```

```
test_images = test_images / 255.0

# Reshape the images to (num_samples, 28, 28)
train_images = train_images.reshape(-1, 28, 28)
test_images = test_images.reshape(-1, 28, 28)
```

Training Loop

After ensuring that both the data and the model are prepared, we move on to the training phase. In this section, we make use of the fit method that is made available by TensorFlow's Keras API. For the sake of demonstration, we will train for a total of ten epochs.

```
history = transformer.fit(train_images, train_labels, epochs=10,
                          batch_size=64, validation_split=0.2)
```

During training, TensorFlow will provide real-time feedback, including the loss and accuracy for both training and validation sets. You can observe how the model improves over epochs.

Model Evaluation

After training, it's time to evaluate the model's performance on the test dataset. This will give us a clear indication of how well the model generalizes to new data.

```
test_loss, test_accuracy = transformer.evaluate(test_images, test_labels)
print("Test accuracy: {:.2f}%".format(test_accuracy * 100))
```

Interpretation and Analysis

The transformer architecture, initially designed for natural language processing tasks, showcases its versatility by performing admirably on the MNIST image classification task. This is particularly remarkable, as it suggests the transformer's capability to adapt to different types of sequence data, whether it be text, images, or even more complex data forms.

In real-world scenarios, the transformer's parallelism and attention mechanisms make it suitable for tasks that require understanding of long-range dependencies, or when the input data doesn't strictly fall into the realm of sequences. This includes tasks like object detection in images, where the spatial relationship between pixels can offer valuable context, or even in stock price prediction, where the temporal relationship between different time points could be crucial.

You have not only trained a transformer model by following these steps, but you have also gained insights into the flexibility and power of the transformer model. You now have a good foundation to build upon when adapting transformers to a diverse range of machine learning problems.

Fine-tuning Transformer Model

Fine-tuning is a potent strategy in machine learning, especially in scenarios where your dataset is not large enough to train a model from scratch effectively. It involves taking a pre-trained model, typically trained on a large dataset, and then further training it (fine-tuning) on a smaller dataset specific to a particular task. The idea is that the pre-trained model has already learned useful features or representations that can be utilized for the new task, thereby improving performance and reducing training time.

Preparing Your Environment

Before beginning the fine-tuning process, you need to make sure that the pre-trained model and the architecture it uses are suitable for the new job. Since we are going to proceed with our transformer model that was trained on the MNIST dataset, let's assume that you have a dataset of hand-written digits that is comparable to MNIST but is smaller. You may have used MNIST for initial training, but now you have a subset of digits that are deemed "difficult to interpret," and you want to fine-tune the model based on these digits.

Fine-Tuning Approach

You can generally choose between two different strategies for fine-tuning. The first option is to stop making changes to the model at the initial layers and instead concentrate on refining the higher-level layers. This is especially helpful in situations in which the new task is significantly dissimilar to the task that the model was initially trained on. The second strategy is to perform extensive adjustments to the model as a whole. This comes in handy in situations in which the new task is extremely similar to the task that was originally assigned. Given that our new dataset is comparable to the previous one but more specific, the transformer model that we developed for MNIST will be fine-tuned making use of the second approach.

```
# Assume fine_tune_images and fine_tune_labels are your new dataset
# Normalize and reshape just like you did with the original MNIST dataset
fine_tune_images = fine_tune_images / 255.0
fine_tune_images = fine_tune_images.reshape(-1, 28, 28)
```

Fine-Tuning Procedure

After preparing the new dataset, the process for fine-tuning is almost exactly the same as the process that was used to train the model in the first place. On the other hand, if you want to prevent the model from forgetting information that is helpful to it, you should consider using a slower learning rate.

```
# Adjust learning rate
new_optimizer = Adam(learning_rate=0.0001)

# Compile the model again
transformer.compile(optimizer=new_optimizer, loss=loss_object, metrics=['accuracy'])

# Fine-tune the model
fine_tune_history = transformer.fit(fine_tune_images, fine_tune_labels, epochs=5,
batch_size=32)
```

Evaluation and Adaptation

After the model has been fine-tuned, it is essential to re-evaluate it utilizing the newly acquired data as well as, if possible, a validation set. The results of this evaluation will shed light on the efficiency with which the process of fine-tuning was carried out.

```
# Evaluate the fine-tuned model
fine_tune_loss, fine_tune_accuracy = transformer.evaluate(fine_tune_images,
fine_tune_labels)
print("Fine-tuned model accuracy: {:.2f}%".format(fine_tune_accuracy * 100))
```

The ability to make minute adjustments to models paves the way for a wide variety of applications in the real world. For instance, in the medical field, a model that has been trained to recognize a wide variety of diseases in X-ray images could be fine-tuned to recognize a rare condition, which would aid in the process of making a diagnosis more quickly. In the world of finance, a model that has been trained to predict stock prices can be fine-tuned to concentrate on a particular industry. Transfer learning, and by extension, fine-tuning, are essential components of modern machine learning for a number of reasons, including the adaptability it provides, which is one of those reasons. It makes it possible to apply high-capacity models to specialized tasks, such as transformers, which frequently results in superior performance when compared to starting from scratch with training.

Text Summarization Techniques

The process of condensing a longer document into a concise and logical summary while preserving the most vital information from that longer document is referred to as text summarization. This is an illustration of a sequence-to-sequence task, which can be found in the context of neural networks and machine learning. The transformer model, which was originally developed for machine translation, is especially well-suited for the process of text summarization. Extractive and abstractive summarization are the two primary approaches to a text's analysis that can be taken.

Extractive Summarization

Extractive summarization techniques work by sifting through the original text to pinpoint and extract whole sentences that encapsulate the essence of the content. This method maintains the integrity of the original sentences, simply cherry-picking those that carry the bulk of the information to form a summary. While this technique might be less demanding on computational resources, it can sometimes lead to summaries that, although coherent, lack brevity and conciseness. One of the primary benefits of extractive summarization is its straightforwardness in implementation, coupled with a high likelihood of producing grammatically sound summaries. To achieve this, algorithms such as TextRank leverage the power of sentence embeddings and other natural language processing techniques to rank and select sentences that are most representative of the text's overall theme.

Abstractive Summarization

Abstractive summarization goes a step further by not just selecting text directly from the source but by allowing the summarization model to creatively paraphrase and even innovate new phrases or entire sentences. This advanced approach is designed to construct summaries that are not only coherent but also succinct, capturing the original text's meaning in a more condensed form. The main challenge here is ensuring that the new, briefer versions preserve the full context and original intent of the source material. Transformer-based models, renowned for their sophisticated attention mechanisms, are particularly adept at abstractive summarization. They have the capability to understand and process the full scope of a document, considering all its nuances, which enables them to generate high-quality summaries that remain true to the source content.

Hybrid Approach

The hybrid summarization approach marries the extractive and abstractive techniques to leverage the strengths of both. In this method, the model starts by utilizing an extractive process to identify and pick out the key sentences that form the backbone of the content. Following this, it employs abstractive methods to rephrase and refine these sentences, ensuring that the final summary is not only coherent and comprehensive but also elegantly presented. This dual-step approach is particularly valuable when dealing with intricate and dense documents where pinpointing the crucial elements and then articulating them in a clear, concise manner is of the utmost importance. This hybrid method ensures that the summaries are both accurate in reflecting the source material and also enjoyable and easy to read, providing a balanced and effective summarization solution.

The architecture often used for text summarization tasks, especially abstractive summarization, is the encoder-decoder model. The encoder processes the input document and compresses the information into a fixed-size context vector. The decoder then takes this vector to generate a summary. Transformer models naturally fit into this encoder-decoder framework. The original transformer model itself is an encoder-decoder model, where the encoder processes the input sequence and the decoder generates the output sequence, both working in tandem.

Text summarization comes with its own set of challenges. One of the primary issues is maintaining the balance between informativeness and conciseness. A summary should be short but must also capture the essence of the document. Another challenge is ensuring the factual accuracy of the summary, especially in abstractive summarization where the model is allowed to generate new sentences. Advanced techniques like reinforcement learning from human feedback (RLHF) are being explored to address these challenges.

Building Abstractive Text Summarization Model

Dataset and Preliminaries

For this demonstration, let's consider using the CNN/Daily Mail dataset, a commonly used dataset for text summarization tasks. The dataset consists of news articles and their respective summaries. You can download it from below URL:
https://cs.nyu.edu/~kcho/DMQA/

Once downloaded, you would typically preprocess the text, tokenize it, and then convert it into sequences of integers. We'll assume that this preprocessing step has been completed.

Model Architecture

An encoder-decoder model that is based on a transformer will serve as the architecture for the abstractive summarization approach that we will take. The text that is provided as input will be processed by the encoder, which will then produce a context vector. After that, the decoder will make use of the context vector in order to produce the summary text. Encoder and decoder will each have multiple layers of transformer units that make up their respective structures. Because the transformer units contain mechanisms for self-attention, this architecture enables the model to effectively manage lengthy sequences. This is due to the fact that the architecture was designed.

Encoder Implementation

The encoder part will comprise multiple layers of transformer units. Each unit will have multi-headed self-attention followed by feed-forward neural networks. Batch normalization and layer normalization will be applied at appropriate stages. Below is a simplified code snippet for creating the encoder using TensorFlow:

```
from tensorflow.keras import layers

class Encoder(layers.Layer):
    def __init__(self, num_layers, d_model, num_heads):
        super(Encoder, self).__init__()
        self.num_layers = num_layers
```

```
    self.enc_layers = [TransformerLayer(d_model, num_heads) for _ in range(num_layers)]

  def call(self, x, training, mask):
    for i in range(self.num_layers):
      x = self.enc_layers[i](x, training, mask)
    return x  # (batch_size, input_seq_len, d_model)
```

Decoder Implementation

In addition to this, the decoder will have several layers of different transformer units. On the other hand, it will feature an additional set of layers in order to conceal its multi-headed attention. Because of this, the decoder is able to concentrate on various aspects of the output produced by the encoder as it generates each word in the summary.

```
class Decoder(layers.Layer):
  def __init__(self, num_layers, d_model, num_heads):
    super(Decoder, self).__init__()
    self.num_layers = num_layers
    self.dec_layers = [TransformerLayer(d_model, num_heads) for _ in range(num_layers)]

  def call(self, x, enc_output, training, look_ahead_mask, padding_mask):
    for i in range(self.num_layers):
      x = self.dec_layers[i](x, enc_output, training, look_ahead_mask, padding_mask)
    return x
```

Training the Model

Once the encoder and decoder are defined, you can proceed to compile and train the model. It's crucial to choose an appropriate loss function and optimizer. Given that this is a sequence-to-sequence task, a common choice for the loss function is categorical cross-entropy.

```
model.compile(optimizer='adam', loss='categorical_crossentropy', metrics=['accuracy'])
model.fit(train_dataset, epochs=20, batch_size=64, validation_data=val_dataset)
```

Model Evaluation and Summary Generation

Following the training phase, you would normally evaluate the model using a separate test set in order to determine how well it performed. In order to generate summaries, you would use a method such as beam search or greedy decoding, which are both designed to convert the output of the decoder into text that is readable by humans.

Bottom Line

The task of summarizing a text, and particularly doing so in an abstractive manner, is one that is both challenging and rewarding. Because it can generate summaries that are both concise and coherent, it has applications in a wide variety of fields, including healthcare, legal firms, and news organizations, among others. It turns out that the transformer-based model, with all of its parallelization and attention mechanisms, is an extremely useful tool for carrying out this activity. Because it can take into account the entire sequence while still coming up with individual words, it is ideally suited for producing summaries of a high caliber. As a result of going through this hands-on exercise, you now have the foundational knowledge necessary to construct, train, and put into practice a text summarization model.

Performance Optimization Techniques

Gradient Clipping

When it comes to optimizing transformer models, gradient clipping is one of the most straightforward techniques available. In the process of training deep neural networks, the gradients that are calculated during backpropagation can experience numerical instability if they become either excessively large or excessively small. The problem in question is referred to as the exploding and vanishing gradients problem. This issue is addressed by the gradient clipping technique, which restricts the gradients to fall within a given range. When training transformer models with a high learning rate or working on tasks that involve long sequences, you will find that it is particularly helpful. Gradient clipping is a technique that, by regulating the gradients, ensures that the model updates are neither excessively large nor excessively small. As a result, the training process is both more consistent and more expedient.

Learning Rate Scheduling

Another essential optimization strategy, known as learning rate scheduling, adjusts the learning rate at various points throughout the training process. There is a possibility that maintaining a constant learning rate will not be productive throughout the training process. In the beginning stages, increasing the learning rate can help to speed up the training process. However, once the model starts to converge, decreasing the learning rate is preferable so that the parameters can be fine-tuned. The original Transformer architecture that was proposed by Vaswani and colleagues made use of a bespoke learning rate scheduler. This scheduler increased the learning rate linearly for a few epochs before beginning to decrease it in a manner that was proportional to the inverse square root of the number of epochs. This dynamic adjustment of the learning rate has the potential to significantly accelerate the convergence, which in turn will improve the model's overall performance.

Layer Normalization

Layer normalization is a strategy that has been shown to be very effective in the past for ensuring the consistency of the training of deep neural networks. When working with transformer models, layer normalization is typically applied after the residual connection and before each sub-layer (such as a feed-forward neural network or self-attention neural network). When the activations of each layer are normalized, it guarantees that they have a consistent mean and standard deviation, which contributes to the stabilization of the training. It also reduces the likelihood of a phenomenon known as internal covariate shift, which occurs when the distribution of activations shifts in the course of training and impedes the rate of learning.

Weight Sharing

Weight sharing is yet another optimization strategy that, in addition to lowering the total number of trainable parameters, has the potential to boost overall performance. Weight sharing is a technique that is frequently utilized in transformer models. This technique is applied between the embedding layer and the pre-softmax linear transformation in the decoder. This particular method of parameter sharing aligns the model's input and output representations and functions as a form of regularization, thereby reducing the likelihood of the model being overfit. Because transformers have a large number of parameters, it is sometimes necessary to employ strategies such as weight sharing in order to effectively train the model. This is especially true when there is a limited amount of data to work with.

Mixed Precision Training

As a result of the frequently large number of parameters and calculations that are involved with transformers, the training can be quite computationally intensive. Mixed precision training requires the use of arithmetic with a lower precision (such as float16 instead of float32) for certain calculations. This lowers the memory requirements and speeds up the training process. Even though not all operations can be performed with a lower degree of precision without risk, many deep learning frameworks, such as TensorFlow and PyTorch, provide simple APIs for training with mixed degrees of precision. The difficulty lies in ensuring that the reduced precision does not negatively affect the performance of the model, which is generally something that modern frameworks for deep learning are able to handle quite well.

Selecting the Right Technique

In order to achieve optimal performance with transformer models, it is necessary to thoughtfully select and combine a variety of optimization approaches. While some approaches are geared toward accelerating the learning process, others are concentrated on enhancing the generalization capability of the model. Because of the complexity of the architecture and the requirements for computational power, efficient optimization is absolutely necessary for successful deployment. It is possible for you to significantly improve the performance and efficiency of your transformer models if you have an understanding of and put into practice a number of well-known optimization techniques.

Apply Learning Rate Scheduling

When it comes to optimization strategies that are effective at stabilizing the training of transformer models, one of the most useful is called learning rate scheduling. In this section, our primary focus will be on the implementation of a custom learning rate scheduler in TensorFlow, one that is analogous to the one that Vaswani et al. initially proposed for the transformer architecture. This scheduler will at first make a linear improvement to the learning rate, and then it will make a reduction in that rate that is proportional to the inverse square root of the epoch number.

Custom Learning Rate Scheduler

To start, let's make a specialized scheduler for our learning rate. The following formula describes the learning rate:

$$\text{Learning Rate} = \min\left(\text{step\_num}^{-0.5}, \text{step\_num} \times \text{warmup\_steps}^{-1.5}\right)$$

Given below is how you can implement this in TensorFlow:

```
import tensorflow as tf

class CustomSchedule(tf.keras.optimizers.schedules.LearningRateSchedule):
  def __init__(self, d_model, warmup_steps=4000):
    super(CustomSchedule, self).__init__()

    self.d_model = d_model
    self.d_model = tf.cast(self.d_model, tf.float32)
    self.warmup_steps = warmup_steps

  def __call__(self, step):
    arg1 = tf.math.rsqrt(step)
    arg2 = step * (self.warmup_steps ** -1.5)

    return tf.math.rsqrt(self.d_model) * tf.math.minimum(arg1, arg2)
```

You can use this custom schedule when compiling your transformer model:

```
learning_rate = CustomSchedule(d_model)
optimizer = tf.keras.optimizers.Adam(learning_rate, beta_1=0.9, beta_2=0.98, epsilon=1e-9)

model.compile(optimizer=optimizer, loss='sparse_categorical_crossentropy',
metrics=['accuracy'])
```

Finally, you can train your model as usual. The learning rate will now change dynamically according to the schedule:

```
model.fit(train_dataset, epochs=20, batch_size=64, validation_data=val_dataset)
```

Evaluating the Impact

After your model has been trained, it is essential to conduct an analysis to determine how the learning rate scheduling has affected the model's overall performance. When compared with another version of the model that was trained without using learning rate scheduling, training loss, validation loss, and other metrics should be analyzed. You should notice that the model converges more quickly, and possibly even achieves a lower validation loss; this demonstrates the efficacy of the optimization technique that you are using.

You are implementing a strategy when you apply learning rate scheduling that not only accelerates the process of training but also has the potential to lead to improved generalization and performance on data that has not been seen before. With the help of this hands-on example, you should have a better understanding of how to effectively apply optimization techniques to transformer model simulations.

Summary

In this chapter, the primary focus was on diving deep into the architecture and optimization techniques of transformer models. Starting with the architectural uniqueness of transformers, we understood how they differ significantly from RNNs and CNNs, especially in handling sequences. The self-attention mechanism was highlighted as a cornerstone, enabling the model to consider the entire context, thereby excelling in tasks like machine translation and summarization. This detailed exploration clarified why transformers are now the go-to architecture for various NLP applications.

We also implemented a transformer model practically, focusing on the encoder and decoder architecture. The hands-on exercise covered the steps from initialization to training, providing a comprehensive understanding of building transformers using TensorFlow. It is this architectural strength, coupled with self-attention mechanisms, that makes transformers powerful for sequence-to-sequence tasks, outperforming older architectures like RNNs and LSTMs in various aspects.

The latter part of the chapter delved into optimization techniques specifically tailored for transformer models. We learned various strategies, from gradient clipping and learning rate scheduling to layer normalization and weight sharing, each with its unique advantages. One of the standout techniques was learning rate scheduling, which we applied practically to our transformer model. This exercise demonstrated how such techniques could improve training efficiency and model performance substantially.

The chapter aimed to offer a balanced mix of theoretical understanding and practical skills. With this knowledge, one should be well-equipped to build, optimize, and understand transformer models for a variety of applications, from text summarization and translation to more complex tasks like question answering and language generation. This blend of theory and practice is critical for anyone aiming to delve deeper into the realm of Natural Language Processing using transformers.

CHAPTER 7: AUTOENCODERS FOR DATA COMPRESSION AND GENERATION

Introduction to Autoencoders

Brief Overview

Autoencoders make up their own distinct subcategory within the larger field of unsupervised machine learning models. These models are employed primarily for the purposes of dimensionality reduction and feature learning. In contrast to conventional supervised learning models, in which the objective is to map inputs to labels, the goal of an autoencoder is to reconstruct its input data in as accurate a manner as is possible given the data that was given to it. Because of this, they are particularly useful for unsupervised tasks such as anomaly detection, denoising, and even, to some extent, generative modeling.

The encoder and the decoder are the two primary parts that make up an autoencoder. The input is then encoded as an internal representation with a fixed size and reduced dimensionality after the encoder has first been used to compress it into a latent-space representation. The decoder will then use this internal representation to piece back together the original input data. The goal of the training is to reduce, as much as possible, the gap between the original input and the output of the reconstruction. The model is able to learn a compressed representation of the input data with this kind of architecture, which serves as an effective form of dimensionality reduction.

Latent Space and Information Bottleneck

The concept of the latent space, often the centerpiece of an autoencoder's architecture, serves as an information bottleneck—a pivotal zone where data is distilled into its most essential attributes. This compressed form of data representation demands that autoencoders distill and retain only the most salient features that are crucial for reconstruction, thereby learning a more efficient representation of the input data. However, the art of defining the dimensionality of this latent space is a delicate balance and a crucial aspect of model configuration. It is a hyperparameter that must be finely tuned, as it dictates the compression level and, by extension, the model's capacity to learn meaningful data representations.

If the latent space is too expansive, the autoencoder may simply learn to act as an identity function, effectively copying its input to its output without learning any meaningful patterns in the data. This oversized latent space can lead to a model that does not generalize well and fails to provide any significant compression or abstraction of the input data. Conversely, a latent space that is too restrictive in its dimensionality can be equally detrimental. In this scenario, the model might become too constrained to encode the necessary information, resulting in a loss of critical data features and a reconstruction that lacks fidelity. Thus, finding the sweet spot for the latent space dimensionality is key—it must be large enough to capture the underlying data distribution and nuances but compact enough to force the model to prioritize and learn the most informative features.

Types of Autoencoders

Autoencoders, as versatile neural network models, can be differentiated into several types, each tailored to tackle different kinds of data and tasks. The range extends from the basic linear autoencoders that are capable of handling straightforward, non-complex relationships within data, to the more sophisticated convolutional autoencoders that excel with image data by leveraging their inherent ability to recognize spatial hierarchies and patterns. On the other hand, recurrent autoencoders stand out when dealing with sequential or time-series data, as they can capture temporal dynamics effectively. The diversity in autoencoder architectures ensures that there is a suitable model for various data dimensions and complexities, allowing for flexibility and precision in unsupervised learning tasks. Each type of autoencoder can be fine-tuned and optimized for specific scenarios, whether it be for dimensionality reduction, feature learning, or even anomaly detection.

Loss Functions and Training

The loss function of an autoencoder is typically some form of reconstruction loss. This loss function measures how well the decoder is doing its job of reconstructing the input data. Mean Squared Error, abbreviated as MSE, is a statistic that is frequently applied here. Using general-purpose optimization algorithms such as Adam or SGD, the model is educated to reduce this reconstruction loss as much as possible.

You will be well-prepared to apply autoencoders in a variety of scenarios that call for feature learning or dimensionality reduction if you have a solid understanding of their architecture and the fundamental principles that drive their operation. They offer a powerful tool for undertaking unsupervised learning tasks, in which they extract the most important features from the data without the need for any labels to be present.

My First Autoencoder!

We shall get started with the same MNIST dataset as Keras makes it simple to gain access to this dataset. Import the data set, then normalize the images by dividing them by 255 to make sure that the values of each pixel are between 0 and 1. Alter the form of the images so that they are suitable for use with the autoencoder's layers, and do this while you are at it.

```
from keras.datasets import mnist
import numpy as np

(x_train, _), (x_test, _) = mnist.load_data()
x_train = x_train.astype('float32') / 255.
x_test = x_test.astype('float32') / 255.
x_train = np.reshape(x_train, (len(x_train), 28, 28, 1))
x_test = np.reshape(x_test, (len(x_test), 28, 28, 1))
```

Designing the Architecture

Encoders and decoders are the two components that make up autoencoders. The input is compressed before being sent to the encoder, which then sends it to the decoder, which attempts to reconstruct it. We shall create a basic autoencoder by utilizing the Sequential API provided by Keras. For the encoder, we'll use Conv2D layers to progressively downsample the image, and for the decoder, we'll use Conv2DTranspose layers to upsample the image so that it returns to its original dimensions.

```
from keras.models import Sequential
from keras.layers import Conv2D, MaxPooling2D, UpSampling2D

autoencoder = Sequential()

# Encoder
autoencoder.add(Conv2D(32, (3, 3), activation='relu', padding='same', input_shape=(28, 28, 1)))
autoencoder.add(MaxPooling2D((2, 2), padding='same'))
autoencoder.add(Conv2D(16, (3, 3), activation='relu', padding='same'))
autoencoder.add(MaxPooling2D((2, 2), padding='same'))
```

```
# Decoder
autoencoder.add(Conv2D(16, (3, 3), activation='relu', padding='same'))
autoencoder.add(UpSampling2D((2, 2)))
autoencoder.add(Conv2D(32, (3, 3), activation='relu', padding='same'))
autoencoder.add(UpSampling2D((2, 2)))
autoencoder.add(Conv2D(1, (3, 3), activation='sigmoid', padding='same'))
```

Compiling and Training the Model

The subsequent step, after defining the architecture, is to compile the model. Since we want to achieve the goal of achieving the smallest possible difference between the images that were input and those that were reconstructed, we will use the Adam optimizer and the mean squared error as the loss function.

```
autoencoder.compile(optimizer='adam', loss='mean_squared_error')
```

The process of training an autoencoder is comparable to training any other type of neural network. When training the model on the MNIST dataset, the fit method should be used.

```
autoencoder.fit(x_train, x_train, epochs=50, batch_size=256, shuffle=True,
validation_data=(x_test, x_test))
```

Evaluating the Model

After the training has been completed, the model should be evaluated by encoding and decoding the test set using it. When evaluating the effectiveness of the model, it is helpful to contrast the original image with the one that was reconstructed. To obtain the reconstructed images, make use of the predict method in Keras.

```
decoded_imgs = autoencoder.predict(x_test)
```

If you want to get an idea of how well your autoencoder is doing, you can compare the reconstructed image to the original one and see the results side by side.

By following these steps, you've successfully built, compiled, and trained a simple autoencoder using Keras.

Sparse Autoencoders

Sparse autoencoders are a subtype of traditional autoencoders. Unlike traditional autoencoders, sparse autoencoders are intended to ensure that only a small percentage of neurons in the hidden layers are activated at any one time. When it comes to standard autoencoders, the primary objective is to minimize the penalty for reconstruction error. On the other hand, sparse autoencoders have an additional term added to the loss function. This term prevents the network from activating an excessive number of neurons, which results in representations that are more "sparse." In essence, this sparsity constraint guarantees that the model will learn more reliable and significant characteristics. Sparsity is frequently desirable because it has the potential to reduce the likelihood of the network overfitting itself and produce a model that is easier to interpret.

Sparsity Regulation Mechanism

In a sparse autoencoder, the activation of neurons in the hidden layer is limited by including a sparsity penalty and a reconstruction error in the loss function. This is done in place of the traditional loss function. The addition of a term to the loss that is proportional to the average activation of each neuron in the hidden layer is the method that is utilized the vast majority of the time when trying to enforce sparsity. In order to calculate the sparsity loss, this average activation is first compared to a sparsity parameter, which is typically a small value that is relatively close to zero.

Modifying the Loss Function

We will modify the loss function so that it includes a sparsity term in order to add sparsity to the autoencoder that we already have. Creating a loss function from scratch in Keras is the way to accomplish this goal. Both the mean squared error term and the sparsity term will be incorporated into the custom loss function that you create. In most cases, this is accomplished by including the Kullback-Leibler (KL) divergence for each neuron in the hidden layer, which compares the target sparsity to the actual sparsity of the data.

Practical Implementation: Adding Sparsity

We shall modify our previous autoencoder to include a sparsity constraint. You don't need to change the architecture; instead, you only need to change the loss function. Below is how you can modify the loss function to include a sparsity term.

```
from keras import regularizers

# Create the sparse autoencoder by adding activity regularizers to the encoder layers
autoencoder_sparse = Sequential()

# Encoder
autoencoder_sparse.add(Conv2D(32, (3, 3), activation='relu', padding='same',
activity_regularizer=regularizers.l1(1e-5), input_shape=(28, 28, 1)))
autoencoder_sparse.add(MaxPooling2D((2, 2), padding='same'))
autoencoder_sparse.add(Conv2D(16, (3, 3), activation='relu', padding='same',
activity_regularizer=regularizers.l1(1e-5)))
autoencoder_sparse.add(MaxPooling2D((2, 2), padding='same'))

# Decoder remains the same as before
autoencoder_sparse.add(Conv2D(16, (3, 3), activation='relu', padding='same'))
autoencoder_sparse.add(UpSampling2D((2, 2)))
autoencoder_sparse.add(Conv2D(32, (3, 3), activation='relu', padding='same'))
autoencoder_sparse.add(UpSampling2D((2, 2)))
autoencoder_sparse.add(Conv2D(1, (3, 3), activation='sigmoid', padding='same'))

# Compile and train the sparse autoencoder
autoencoder_sparse.compile(optimizer='adam', loss='mean_squared_error')
autoencoder_sparse.fit(x_train, x_train, epochs=50, batch_size=256, shuffle=True,
validation_data=(x_test, x_test))
```

Analysis and Comparison

After training, you will be able to examine the differences between the features that were learned by the standard autoencoder and those that were learned by the sparse autoencoder. In most cases, you will discover that the sparse autoencoder has learned a greater number of distinguishing characteristics. As a result of the sparsity constraint, the model is compelled to zero in on the most prominent characteristics of the input data, which in most cases leads to improved generalization performance on data that has not previously been examined.

By gaining an understanding of sparse autoencoders and putting them into practice, you are expanding your toolkit for unsupervised learning. You now have access to a new method that not only decreases the dimensionality of the data, but does so in a way that draws attention to the aspects of the data that are most significant.

Explore Variational Autoencoders

Variational autoencoders, also known as VAEs, are a particular kind of autoencoder that incorporate a probabilistic component into the model. VAEs, in contrast to traditional autoencoders, map an input to a distribution in the latent space. Traditional autoencoders, on the other hand, map an input to a fixed latent space. Because of this, VAEs are able to generate new samples that are comparable to the training data; as a result, they are an excellent tool for generative tasks. The architecture is comprised of an encoder, a decoder, and a loss function that is somewhat more complicated than those found in conventional autoencoders. A term that evaluates how well the model reconstructs the input data and a term that evaluates how closely the latent variables match a prior distribution, which is typically a standard normal distribution, are both included in the loss function.

Probabilistic Mapping

In VAEs, the encoder doesn't directly produce a point in the latent space. Instead, it produces the parameters of a probability distribution—typically, the mean and standard deviation of a Gaussian distribution. The latent vector is then sampled from this distribution. This stochastic element ensures that points that are close in the original space will also be close in the latent space, which is ideal for generative models.

Generating New Data

The decoder of a VAE works the same way as a standard autoencoder. It takes a point from the latent space and maps it back to the original data space. The key difference is that this point doesn't have to be a point that was encoded from the training set. It can be any point in the latent space, allowing VAEs to generate new data that is similar to but not exactly the same as the training data.

Reconstruction and Regularization

The dual-component loss function of VAEs is what guides them to be effective generative models. The first component is the reconstruction loss, which is responsible for how accurately the model can replicate the input data. This part of the loss function typically utilizes measures like the mean squared error or binary cross-entropy to quantify reconstruction accuracy. The second component is the regularization term, which aligns the encoded latent variables with a predefined distribution, usually a standard normal distribution. This is quantified by the Kullback-Leibler (KL) divergence, which measures the difference between the two distributions. The delicate balance between these two parts of the loss function is what ensures that VAEs not only recreate the input data but also generalize well, allowing them to generate new, high-fidelity data.

Sample Program: Building VAE

We shall get familiar with TensorFlow by constructing a basic VAE. We will proceed under the assumption that TensorFlow has already been installed as explained in earlier chapters. To begin, import the required modules as follows:

```
import tensorflow as tf
from tensorflow.keras.layers import Input, Dense, Lambda
from tensorflow.keras.models import Model
```

We shall move on to defining the encoder. The mean and standard deviation of the Gaussian distribution in the latent space will be output by this:

```
input_img = Input(shape=(784,))
hidden_1 = Dense(256, activation='relu')(input_img)
```

```
hidden_2 = Dense(128, activation='relu')(hidden_1)
z_mean = Dense(2)(hidden_2)
z_log_var = Dense(2)(hidden_2)
```

Next, use these parameters to sample a point in the latent space:

```
def sampling(args):
    z_mean, z_log_var = args
    epsilon = tf.random.normal(shape=(tf.shape(z_mean)[0], 2))
    return z_mean + tf.exp(0.5 * z_log_var) * epsilon

z = Lambda(sampling)([z_mean, z_log_var])
```

Now define the decoder:

```
decoder_h1 = Dense(128, activation='relu')
decoder_h2 = Dense(256, activation='relu')
decoder_mean = Dense(784, activation='sigmoid')
h_decoded_1 = decoder_h1(z)
h_decoded_2 = decoder_h2(h_decoded_1)
x_decoded_mean = decoder_mean(h_decoded_2)
```

Finally, construct and compile the VAE model:

```
vae = Model(input_img, x_decoded_mean)
xent_loss = tf.keras.losses.mse(input_img, x_decoded_mean)
kl_loss = - 0.5 * tf.reduce_mean(1 + z_log_var - tf.square(z_mean) - tf.exp(z_log_var))
vae_loss = xent_loss + kl_loss
vae.add_loss(vae_loss)
vae.compile(optimizer='adam')
```

The steps required to train a VAE are identical to those required to train a conventional autoencoder. When you are training the network to reconstruct the input data, you will use your training data in both the input and the target phases of the training process. Following training, you will be able to generate new data by taking samples of points from the latent space and then passing those samples through the decoder.

Image Denoising with Autoencoders

The use of autoencoders in image denoising is a particularly interesting application of these devices. The purpose of this exercise is to teach the autoencoder to map images of noisy digits to images of clean digits. Once the autoencoder has been trained, the idea is that it will have learned to "ignore" the noise and encode the most important features of the input image, thereby removing the noise from the image. This will occur once the autoencoder has been trained. After that, the decoder will be able to reassemble the original, noise-free image from the representation of the image that has been encoded with no noise.

Why Autoencoders for Image Denoising?

Autoencoders have demonstrated tremendous promise as a tool for the process of image denoising. Because of their capability to learn optimized features and to reconstruct input data from a compressed internal state, they are particularly effective in this domain. Any deviation from the learned manifold of clean images is regarded as noise by the autoencoder, which can be trained to learn it. This makes autoencoders more resistant to noisy input, which enables them to reconstruct images that have been cleaned up and denoised.

Types of Noise in Images

It is essential that we recognize that there are many distinct manifestations of noise before we move on to the implementation of this strategy in practice. It could be Gaussian noise, salt-and-pepper noise, or even more complex structured noise like text overlays. Other types of noise include salt-and-pepper noise. The architecture of the autoencoder can be modified to offer improved performance in a manner that is responsive to the nature and intensity of the noise.

Preparing Noisy Images

We shall pretend for the sake of this demonstration that we are working with the MNIST dataset again, which is also easily accessible within TensorFlow.

```
(train_data, _), (test_data, _) = tf.keras.datasets.mnist.load_data()
```

```
train_data = train_data.astype('float32') / 255.
test_data = test_data.astype('float32') / 255.

noise_factor = 0.5
train_data_noisy = train_data + noise_factor * np.random.normal(loc=0.0, scale=1.0,
size=train_data.shape)
test_data_noisy = test_data + noise_factor * np.random.normal(loc=0.0, scale=1.0,
size=test_data.shape)
```

Building the Denoising Autoencoder

We shall construct the autoencoder. The architecture can remain mostly the same as a regular autoencoder, but you'll be training it differently. The following is an example of some code that can be used to create a basic denoising autoencoder with TensorFlow:

```
from tensorflow.keras.layers import Conv2D, MaxPooling2D, UpSampling2D
from tensorflow.keras.models import Sequential

autoencoder = Sequential()

# Encoder
autoencoder.add(Conv2D(32, (3, 3), activation='relu', padding='same', input_shape=(28, 28, 1)))
autoencoder.add(MaxPooling2D((2, 2), padding='same'))

# Decoder
autoencoder.add(Conv2D(32, (3, 3), activation='relu', padding='same'))
autoencoder.add(UpSampling2D((2, 2)))
autoencoder.add(Conv2D(1, (3, 3), activation='sigmoid', padding='same'))

autoencoder.compile(optimizer='adam', loss='mean_squared_error')
```

Training and Evaluation

Training the autoencoder involves feeding the noisy images as input and the clean images as the output. Post-training, you can input a new noisy image to get the denoised version as output.

```
autoencoder.fit(train_data_noisy, train_data, epochs=50, batch_size=256, shuffle=True,
validation_data=(test_data_noisy, test_data))
```

After you have trained the model, you will be able to use it to remove noise from other images that are similar. This has a wide variety of applications, ranging from the cleaning and restoration of documents to the analysis of medical images, where the removal of noise can significantly help with diagnosis. Image denoising can be accomplished with the help of autoencoders using a method that is powerful, data-driven, and does not require manual feature engineering or in-depth knowledge of the domain.

Summary

This chapter presented a comprehensive analysis of autoencoders, beginning with learning their fundamentals before moving on to an examination of more specialized types, including sparse and variational autoencoders. We were shown how autoencoders are able to effectively encode the most important aspects of the data in a form with a reduced number of dimensions. Variational autoencoders, also known as VAEs, take this concept one step further by adding a probabilistic layer. This gives them the ability to generate new data that is analogous to the data that was used for training. This opens up new possibilities for generative models, but it also adds another layer of complexity to the equation.

After that, we shifted our attention to the actual applications of autoencoders in the process of image denoising. The process of understanding the architecture and training process of denoising autoencoders helped shed light on how these neural networks can clean up noisy data, which is a critical preprocessing step in many machine learning pipelines. This chapter demonstrated that autoencoders can learn to filter out noise by training on a dataset that contains both clean and noisy images corresponding to those clean images. This allows the autoencoders to reconstruct clean images. The training procedure was broken down into its component parts and thoroughly explained, including the function of the loss function and its part in directing the network to learn representations free of noise.

This chapter also touched on the adaptability of autoencoders, learning how they can be adapted to different kinds of noise and various applications, ranging from the restoration of documents to medical imaging. The theoretical ideas were driven home with the help of some practical code examples, which also offered a more hands-on method for getting a handle on autoencoders. In order to maintain coherence throughout the book, practical examples were coded in TensorFlow. This made it possible for you to easily incorporate the aforementioned strategies into larger machine learning workflows.

This chapter provided a deeper understanding of autoencoders by elaborating on their theoretical foundations, presenting a variety of autoencoders, and learning their applications in the real world. It provided the conceptual depth as well as the practical know-how necessary to implement autoencoders for tasks ranging from dimensionality reduction to image denoising. As a result, it is an invaluable resource for anyone who is interested in delving into this fascinating area of neural networks.

CHAPTER 8: CAPSULE NETWORKS

Introduction to Capsule Networks

We shall take a quick look at the neural network architectures that we've learned up until this point before we dive headfirst into the fascinating world of Capsule Networks. We began with feedforward neural networks, which are the most basic type of artificial neural networks (ANNs) and are characterized by the absence of any cycle-forming connections between the network's nodes. They are especially helpful for problems involving classification and regression that are relatively straightforward. After that, we dove into the world of convolutional neural networks, also known as CNNs, which are the workhorses of computer vision tasks. CNNs make use of convolutional layers to automatically and adaptively learn spatial hierarchies of features, which enables them to perform extremely well in a variety of tasks, including image classification and object detection, among others.

On the other hand, Recurrent Neural Networks, also known as RNNs, perform exceptionally well when it comes to processing sequences of data. We saw how they can be utilized in time-series prediction, natural language processing, and other tasks that require memory of previous events in order to predict future ones. LSTMs and GRUs are two examples of variants of RNNs that offer solutions to the vanishing gradient problem, which makes it possible to effectively manage lengthy sequences of data. We were first exposed to more advanced architectural concepts by means of transformers and GANs. GANs gave us a taste of unsupervised learning capabilities by generating new, synthetic instances of data that can pass for real data. While Transformers revolutionized the field of Natural Language Processing with their attention mechanisms, GANs gave us a taste of unsupervised learning capabilities.

We shall learn about Capsule Networks, also known as CapsNets, which is a relatively new architecture that was presented by Geoffrey Hinton, Alex Krizhevsky, and Sida Wang in the year 2011. It is the goal of Capsule Networks to overcome some of the limitations of CNNs, particularly with regard to the ability to comprehend spatial hierarchies between objects of varying degrees of complexity. CNNs have proven to be highly successful in a number of computer vision tasks; however, they are inherently flawed in their ability to take into account important spatial hierarchies between objects that are simple and complex. Here is where Capsule Networks can be of assistance to you.

Basics of Capsule Networks

When compared to traditional neural networks, capsule networks represent a paradigm shift because they replace neurones with structures that are called capsules. A group of neurones is embodied within a capsule, and these neurones work together to process information in a synergistic manner to identify objects and the various characteristics they possess within an image. These attributes could encompass a wide variety of properties, such as pose (which incorporates position, size, and orientation), texture, hue, and even more distinguishing features. The distinctive feature of a capsule is the form that its output takes, which is a vector. The magnitude of the vector represents the likelihood that the object that the capsule is intended to detect is present, while the direction of the vector encodes the characteristics of the object.

The Squashing Function

To manage the output of each capsule, a non-linear "squashing" function is utilized. This function is designed to compress the length of the output vector to a range between 0 and 1, indicating the existence likelihood of the object without altering the vector's direction. This squashing process is vital for maintaining the representational integrity of the object's properties within the network.

Dynamic Routing

Dynamic routing stands as a cornerstone innovation in the design of Capsule Networks. Unlike the static architecture of conventional neural networks, dynamic routing bestows upon capsules the autonomy to determine the destination of their outputs. This functionality empowers the network to craft more nuanced part-to-whole relationships, which significantly enhances its comprehension of spatial hierarchies within the data it processes.

Inverse Graphics

Capsule Networks are also notable for their capability reminiscent of inverse graphics operations. Standard graphics practices involve rendering three-dimensional scenes into two-dimensional images. In a captivating reversal of this process, Capsule Networks endeavor to extrapolate the three-dimensional scene parameters from two-dimensional inputs, an ambitious and complex task that holds much promise in the field of artificial intelligence.

Why Capsule Networks?

The major advantage of Capsule Networks is their ability to understand the spatial and hierarchical relationships in an image with fewer data and parameters. They are robust against the variations in the pose of the same object across different images. This makes them ideal for tasks where spatial hierarchies are crucial, such as object segmentation and detection.

The primary strengths of Capsule Networks lie in their proficiency in discerning spatial and hierarchical relationships within imagery data, doing so with a smaller dataset and fewer parameters compared to traditional methods. Their resilience in recognizing variations in the presentation of objects, regardless of the pose changes between different images, positions them as a powerful tool for tasks where understanding spatial hierarchies is paramount, including but not limited to object segmentation and precise detection. While Capsule Networks offer a lot of promise, they are not without limitations. Training a Capsule Network is computationally expensive, and the dynamic routing mechanism can be hard to optimize.

Implement Capsules with TensorFlow

For demonstration purposes, let's again refer the same MNIST dataset. This dataset has been loaded and preprocessed in earlier chapters, so at this point we will jump right into putting the Capsule Network into action.

Defining Capsules

It is possible to use a TensorFlow capsule as a layer in some situations. Squash functions and dynamic routing are two of the primary components that go into making a capsule layer's transformation of an input tensor into an output tensor possible. Because TensorFlow 2.x does not come with a Capsule layer pre-installed, we will have to create our own from the ground up. By subclassing the tf.keras.layers.Layer base class, we will create a custom layer. The dynamic routing algorithm as well as the squashing function will be implemented when the call method is used.

```
import tensorflow as tf

class CapsuleLayer(tf.keras.layers.Layer):
  def __init__(self, num_capsules, dim_vector, num_routing=3, **kwargs):
    super(CapsuleLayer, self).__init__(**kwargs)
    self.num_capsules = num_capsules
    self.dim_vector = dim_vector
    self.num_routing = num_routing
    self.kernel_initializer = 'glorot_uniform'
```

```
def build(self, input_shape):
    self.W = self.add_weight(shape=[self.num_capsules, input_shape[1], self.dim_vector],
                             initializer=self.kernel_initializer,
                             name='W')

def squash(self, s):
    s_norm = tf.norm(s, axis=-1, keepdims=True)
    return (s_norm / (1 + s_norm ** 2)) * s

def call(self, inputs):
    # Implementing the routing algorithm and squashing function here
    # This is a simplified example, the actual implementation can be more complex
```

Building Model

Now that the capsule layer has been defined, we can construct a Capsule Network in TensorFlow by using either the Sequential API or the Functional API. In most cases, the construction of a Capsule Network begins with the application of a convolutional layer for the purpose of feature extraction, which is then followed by one or more capsule layers.

```
model = tf.keras.Sequential([
    tf.keras.layers.Conv2D(64, (9, 9), activation='relu', input_shape=(28, 28, 1)),
    CapsuleLayer(num_capsules=8, dim_vector=16),
    CapsuleLayer(num_capsules=10, dim_vector=16),
    # Output layers
])
```

Model Training

Training a Capsule Network is similar to training any other neural network in TensorFlow. You compile the model, specify the loss function and optimizer, and then call the fit method.

```
model.compile(optimizer='adam', loss='sparse_categorical_crossentropy', metrics=['accuracy'])
```

```
model.fit(x_train, y_train, epochs=10, batch_size=32, validation_data=(x_val, y_val))
```

Following is a quick summary of steps to construct a Capsule Network using TensorFlow:

- Initialize the model using the Sequential or Functional API. These APIs provide a clear and structured way to stack layers linearly or define complex models with shared layers, multiple inputs, or outputs.

- Start with a convolutional layer that uses a kernel size of 9x9, which is commonly adopted in Capsule Networks for capturing a larger receptive field. An activation function like ReLU is applied for introducing non-linearity to the model.

- Define the capsule layers with a specified number of capsules and a dimensional vector that represents the instantiation parameters of a particular entity in the image, such as position, size, orientation, and texture.

- Stack multiple capsule layers if necessary. Each layer captures different levels of abstraction and feature representation, thus allowing the network to learn a hierarchy of features.

- Optionally, add output layers tailored to the specific task at hand, whether it is classification, regression, or something else.

To summarize, when using TensorFlow to implement Capsule Networks, you will need to define a custom layer that encapsulates the logic for squashing and dynamic routing. After that, the layer is incorporated into a model, which, just like any other type of neural network, can be compiled and trained. Capsule Networks are a worthy addition to your machine learning toolkit because, despite their complexity, they offer a powerful tool for capturing spatial and hierarchical relationships in data, making them a worthy addition to your toolkit.

Training Capsule Networks

The Importance of Proper Initialization and Optimization

When compared to training other kinds of neural networks, the process of training a capsule network can have some unique characteristics. Both the initialization of capsule parameters and the selection of optimization algorithms have the potential to have a significant impact on the learning effectiveness of the model. When beginning the training process, it is common practice to begin with an initialization technique such as Xavier or Glorot. There is a good chance that optimization algorithms like Adam or RMSprop will work effectively, but you are free to experiment with a variety of others to find the one that is best suited to your particular issue.

Compilation of the Capsule Network

You are required to compile the Capsule Network before beginning training on it. During compilation, the model must be configured with the selected optimization algorithm, the loss function must be defined, and the metrics to be observed must be chosen. In most cases, the loss function for a Capsule Network will consist of a margin loss, which has been developed especially for this architecture. By subclassing the tf.keras.losses.Loss class, it is possible to implement one's own unique loss functions.

```
from tensorflow.keras.optimizers import Adam

# Compiling the model
model.compile(optimizer=Adam(), loss='categorical_crossentropy', metrics=['accuracy'])
```

Data Augmentation and Regularization

Even though capsule networks typically have fewer parameters than CNNs, they are still susceptible to overfitting on datasets that are too small. Methods such as data augmentation have the potential to be an effective defense mechanism against overfitting. Using TensorFlow's ImageDataGenerator, you can quickly and easily set up a pipeline for the augmentation of data.

Training Schedule and Callbacks

When developing a robust training schedule, it is common practice to dynamically adjust the learning rate based on the performance of the validation. This technique is also referred to as scheduling or learning rate annealing. TensorFlow offers a number of callbacks that can be used to modify the learning rate while the model is being trained. These callbacks can be passed to the fit method in the form of the callbacks argument.

Fitting the Model to Data

During training, the model is provided with the training data as well as the labels that correspond to those data. In addition to that, you will need to specify the batch size as well as the number of epochs. The model will iterate over the training data using the fit method, and it will adjust the capsule parameters based on the computed loss as a result of each iteration.

```
# Fitting the model
history = model.fit(x_train, y_train, epochs=10, batch_size=32, validation_data=(x_val, y_val))
```

Another thing is that it is crucial to monitor not just the loss but also other performance metrics like accuracy, precision, and recall, especially on the validation set. These metrics provide a more rounded view of how well the model is learning the task. TensorFlow allows you to visualize these metrics in real-time using TensorBoard, which can be incredibly useful for long training runs.

Early Stopping and Model Checkpointing

Early stopping is a strategy that can be implemented to prevent overfitting and conserve computational resources. The training process will be terminated early if the performance of the model on the validation set does not improve after a predetermined number of epochs have passed. In addition to this, you should also consider saving the model parameters at the point in time when the validation performance is at its highest. This process, which is referred to as model checkpointing, is simple to implement in TensorFlow by making use of callbacks.

In a nutshell, training a Capsule Network involves a number of nuanced steps that call for careful consideration on the part of the trainer. Each step is essential to the successful training of the model; from initializing the network parameters to selecting the appropriate optimization strategies and monitoring the training process, these are just some of the steps that are involved. Although they are computationally intensive, Capsule Networks have shown promise in a variety of tasks that require an understanding of spatial hierarchies. Because of this, they should be considered an essential tool in the arsenal of any machine learning practitioner.

Object Recognition Using Capsule Networks

Adding Final Layers

The next essential step, which comes after defining and compiling your Capsule Network, is to adjust it so that it can perform object recognition tasks. When learning the MNIST dataset, the term "object recognition" refers to the process of determining which digit from 0 to 9 a particular image depicts. In the case of MNIST, the very last layer of your Capsule Network should have exactly the same number of capsules as there are classes, which is 10. These capsules will each become experts in recognizing a different one of the digits. A probability score that indicates the presence of each digit can be calculated by using the length of the output vector produced by each capsule.

Routing-by-Agreement Mechanism

When performing tasks involving object recognition, the "Routing-by-Agreement" mechanism becomes particularly important. This procedure makes it possible for lower-level capsules to transmit their outputs to higher-level capsules whose inputs "agree" with those outputs. In its most basic form, it can be thought of as a voting system in which lower-level features (such as edges or corners) cast their votes for the presence of higher-level features (such as a complete digit). Capsule Networks are particularly useful for object recognition tasks such as MNIST digit recognition because of the routing-by-agreement mechanism, which enables the network to recognize digits in various poses and deformations.

Model Adaptation for MNIST

We are going to keep the architecture straightforward for MNIST. Assume that the existing model uses convolutional layers to detect features and capsule layers to learn higher-level features. Add one capsule for each digit, making a total of ten capsules for the final Capsule layer. In addition to this, a "Length" layer should be included. This layer should compute the lengths of each of the 10 capsule vectors and then convert those lengths into probability scores.

```
from keras import layers, models
from keras.utils import to_categorical

# Add the final Capsule layer for 10 classes
```

```
model.add(CapsuleLayer(num_capsules=10, dim_vector=16, num_routing=3))

# Add a layer to compute the length of each capsule vector
model.add(layers.Lambda(lambda x: tf.norm(x, axis=-1)))

# Final compilation
model.compile(optimizer='adam', loss='categorical_crossentropy', metrics=['accuracy'])
```

Training the Model for Object Recognition

We'll train the adapted model using the MNIST data. Assume that x_train and y_train are your training data and labels, respectively, and they have been preprocessed appropriately. Given that the loss function is categorical cross-entropy, make sure to one-hot encode the labels.

```
y_train_one_hot = to_categorical(y_train, num_classes=10)

# Training
model.fit(x_train, y_train_one_hot, epochs=10, batch_size=32, validation_split=0.2)
```

Evaluation and Interpretation

After the training is complete, you should assess how well the model performed on the test set. Because Capsule Networks are so complicated, the evaluation process might take significantly longer than it does for models as straightforward as CNNs. However, the additional computational cost is frequently justified when considering the robustness against affine transformations and other types of data deformations. Investigate the confusion matrix in addition to other metrics in order to determine the areas in which the model excels and the areas in which it may be lacking. Overall, when this particular modeling is executed correctly, these Capsule Networks can yield state-of-the-art performance on object recognition tasks, and can contribute a valuable addition to your machine learning toolkit for such applications.

Common Errors and Solutions

Issue: Exploding and Vanishing Gradients

Capsule Networks involve a series of complex operations, including squashing functions and dynamic routing, that can lead to the issue of exploding or vanishing gradients. Exploding gradients can cause numerical instability, while vanishing gradients can make the network untrainable.

Solution:
Gradient Clipping: This involves setting a threshold value for gradients during backpropagation. Any gradient exceeding this value is set to the threshold.

```
optimizer = tf.keras.optimizers.Adam(clipvalue=0.5)
model.compile(optimizer=optimizer, loss='categorical_crossentropy')
```

Weight Regularization: L1 or L2 regularization can be added to the capsule layers to constrain their learning.

```
from keras.regularizers import l2

model.add(CapsuleLayer(num_capsules=10, dim_vector=16, num_routing=3,
kernel_regularizer=l2(0.01)))
```

Issue: Overfitting

Even though Capsule Networks have fewer parameters than CNNs, they can still overfit if trained on insufficient data.

Solution:
Data Augmentation: We've learned this in previous chapters; however, it's worth mentioning again for its importance in combating overfitting.

```
from tensorflow.keras.preprocessing.image import ImageDataGenerator
```

```
datagen = ImageDataGenerator(rotation_range=15, width_shift_range=0.1,
height_shift_range=0.1)
datagen.fit(x_train)
```

Dropout: Although not very common in CapsNet architectures, dropout can still be applied in the fully connected layers before the capsule layers.

```
model.add(layers.Dropout(0.5))
```

Issue: Long Training Times

Capsule Networks involve iterative routing processes that are computationally expensive, which can lead to long training times.

Solution:
Batch Normalization: This can make the network converge faster, thereby reducing training time.

```
model.add(layers.BatchNormalization())
```

Hardware Acceleration: Using a powerful GPU can significantly reduce training time. Make sure to install the GPU version of TensorFlow.

Issue: Class Imbalance

In certain applications, the dataset may have a class imbalance that can make the network biased towards the majority class.

Solution:
Class Weights: TensorFlow allows you to set class weights during the training phase to handle imbalance.

```
class_weights = {0: 1., 1: 5., 2: 2., ...}
model.fit(x_train, y_train, class_weight=class_weights)
```

Undersampling and Oversampling: These are traditional techniques to balance the classes in your dataset before training.

Issue. Insufficient Model Evaluation

Sometimes, just looking at training accuracy isn't enough to evaluate the model's performance.

Solution:
Cross-Validation: K-Fold Cross-Validation can provide a more robust evaluation of the model.

```
from sklearn.model_selection import KFold

kfold = KFold(n_splits=5, shuffle=True)
```

Multiple Metrics: Besides accuracy, consider metrics like F1-score, precision, and recall for a comprehensive evaluation.

```
model.compile(optimizer='adam', loss='categorical_crossentropy', metrics=['accuracy',
'Precision', 'Recall'])
```

Issue: Model Interpretability

Capsule Networks are complex models, and understanding why they make a certain prediction can be challenging.

Solution:
Saliency Maps: These are visualizations of the gradients with respect to the input, showing which parts of the input are most important for making a particular prediction.

Capsule Visualization: You can visualize the activation of individual capsules to understand what features they have learned to detect.

Issue: Hyperparameter Tuning

Capsule Networks come with their set of hyperparameters like the number of capsules, dimensions of capsules, and the number of routing iterations. Setting them incorrectly could lead to sub-optimal performance.

Solution:
Grid Search: You can perform a grid search over a range of hyperparameter values to find the best combination.

```
from sklearn.model_selection import GridSearchCV
from keras.wrappers.scikit_learn import KerasClassifier

# Define parameter grid
param_grid = {'num_capsules': [8, 10], 'dim_vector': [16, 32], 'num_routing': [3, 5]}

# Wrap Keras model
model = KerasClassifier(build_fn=create_capsnet_model, epochs=10, batch_size=32)

# Perform grid search
grid = GridSearchCV(estimator=model, param_grid=param_grid)
grid_result = grid.fit(x_train, y_train)
```

Random Search: Sometimes, it's more effective than grid search for high-dimensional hyperparameter spaces.

```
from sklearn.model_selection import RandomizedSearchCV

# Perform random search
random_search = RandomizedSearchCV(estimator=model, param_distributions=param_grid,
n_iter=50)
random_result = random_search.fit(x_train, y_train)
```

Issue: Capsule Collapse

Sometimes, during training, some capsules may end up not encoding any meaningful information. This phenomenon is known as "capsule collapse."
Solution:

Regularization: Adding regularization terms to the loss function can mitigate this issue.

```
loss = margin_loss + 0.0005 * regularizer_loss
```

Modified Routing Algorithm: Researchers have proposed variations of the routing-by-agreement algorithm to tackle capsule collapse.

Issue: Difficulty in Model Debugging

Debugging a Capsule Network can be challenging due to its inherent complexity.

Solution:
TensorBoard: TensorFlow's TensorBoard can help you monitor various metrics and visualize the computational graph, helping you debug your model.

```
tensorboard_callback = tf.keras.callbacks.TensorBoard(log_dir="./logs")
model.fit(x_train, y_train, epochs=10, callbacks=[tensorboard_callback])
```

Model Summary and Plot: Always print the model summary and even plot the model architecture to understand what's going on.

```
model.summary()
tf.keras.utils.plot_model(model, to_file='model_plot.png', show_shapes=True,
show_layer_names=True)
```

These are some of the most common challenges you may face while working with Capsule Networks. However, armed with this quick handy solutions, you should be well-prepared to tackle these issues head-on.

Summary

We have delved deeply into the world of Capsule Networks (CapsNets) in this chapter. Capsule Networks are a revolutionary innovation that seek to overcome the limitations that are inherent in conventional CNNs. Because CapsNets have the potential to maintain spatial hierarchies between different types of objects, including simple and complex ones, they are ideally suited for applications such as object recognition. This chapter began by providing an explanation of the fundamental architecture of CapsNets, putting an emphasis on the unique way in which they maintain spatial and hierarchical relationships. We became familiar with the mechanism for dynamic routing, the functions of squashing, and the significance of the "capsules" themselves in the process of data encoding.

Additionally, we built a CapsNet from scratch using TensorFlow, which gave us valuable hands-on experience. Each step, from establishing the architecture to preparing the data, was painstakingly explained to lead you through the bewildering yet fascinating structure of CapsNets. From setting up the architecture to preparing the data. Even the training phase was investigated, during which we gained an understanding of essential components such as the Margin Loss function, which is exclusive to Capsule Networks. This chapter will walk you through a real-world example, specifically object recognition using the MNIST dataset, to demonstrate the usefulness of CapsNets in practical settings.

In spite of this, the chapter does not shy away from learning the potential pitfalls and difficulties that one might face when working with CapsNets. One of these was hyperparameter tuning, another was capsule collapse, and a third was the inherent complexity that makes debugging difficult. Practical solutions, which were frequently accompanied by code snippets, were provided in order to address these issues. These solutions ranged from grid and random search techniques for hyperparameter optimization to regularization strategies for preventing capsule collapse.

The chapter also dedicated a considerable portion to fine-tuning and optimization techniques. Whether it was about understanding the intricacies of the routing algorithm or learning to use TensorFlow's TensorBoard for effective debugging, the aim was to equip you with a well-rounded understanding of Capsule Networks. With a balance of theoretical knowledge and practical skills, this chapter serves as a comprehensive walkthrough to CapsNets and their application in modern machine learning tasks.

Thank You

Index

S

T

U

V

W

Epilogue

Let's take a moment to reflect on the journey we've been through together in this book. We started as beginners, curious about the world of neural networks and Python, and now we're wrapping up with a toolbox full of skills and a mind brimming with knowledge, ready to tackle the world of machine learning.

Think back to when we first learned about those straightforward networks, piecing together layers like building blocks, and then stepped into the world of TensorFlow and Keras. It was like learning a new language—a language that let us speak to computers and breathe life into our data.

Then came the game-changer: GANs. These networks didn't just recognize stuff; they made stuff up, like a painter with a canvas but in the form of algorithms. And transformers? They showed us a whole new way to handle words and sentences, breaking free from the slow, one-word-at-a-time approach.

By the time we hit capsule networks, we weren't just playing with code; we were shaping it to understand images like a human brain might, with depth and context.

This book wasn't just about coding; it was about understanding the "why" behind it all. And that's the part that sticks with you, even as tech keeps racing ahead. We've been on a ride that's taught us not just to follow instructions but to think, adapt, and maybe even one day lead the charge in new AI adventures.

As we close this book, think of it not as the end but as the first big step into a much larger world. The world of AI is huge and always changing, and you're now equipped to jump in and make your mark.

So, what's next? That's up to you. Go out there and solve problems, dream up new ideas, and keep on learning. The future's looking exciting, and you're ready to be part of it.

The adventure is just beginning!

www.ingramcontent.com/pod-product-compliance
Lightning Source LLC
Chambersburg PA
CBHW080214170726
48282CB00030B/1116
* 9 7 8 8 1 1 9 1 7 7 4 8 6 *